CACTI
of the Desert Southwest
MEG QUINN

Rio Nuevo Publishers
Tucson, Arizona

Rio Nuevo Publishers
An imprint of Treasure Chest Books
P.O. Box 5250
Tucson, AZ 85703-0250

© 2001 Meg Quinn
All Rights Reserved

No part of this publication may be reproduced, stored or introduced into a retrieval system, or likewise copied in any form without the prior written permission of the publisher, excepting quotes for review or citation.

Editor: Ronald J. Foreman
Designer: William Benoit, Simpson & Convent

Photographs
© David Bertelsen: 8, 13, 46, 63 (top)
© Russ Bishop: 47
© Michael Chamberland: 3, 10, 28, 31, 45, 61, 63 (bottom), 67, 68, 69, 71, 82
© Carr Clifton: Title page
© Susan E. Degginger: 11, 52, 53, 60,
© Mark Dimmitt: 19 (top), 23, 54, 64, 76 (both), 80 (top)
© John Dittli: 62
© Douglas B. Evans: 1, 6, 7, 16, 26, 29, 36, 41, 42, 44, 86
© George M. Ferguson: 66
© A.H. Guhl: 12, 15, 25, 34, 48, 55, 65, 79
© Jim Hills: 75 (top)
© Jim Honcoop: iii, viii, 2, 4 (both), 20, 35, 56, 57, 59, 64, 72, 74, 78, 80 (bottom), 81, 83
© George H.H. Huey: Cover, 22
© Lorena Babcock Moore: 9
© William A Pluemer: 24, 39, 50
© Meg Quinn: 15, 17, 18, 19 (bottom), 21, 30, 38, 43, 49, 51, 70, 73, 75, 77
© Scott T. Smith: 27
© David H. Smith: 5
© Jon Mark Stewart: 14, 33, 37, 40, 58

Library of Congress Cataloging-in-Publication Data

Quinn, Meg.
    Cacti of the Desert Southwest / Meg Quinn.
       p. cm.
Includes bibliographical references.
    ISBN 1-887896-28-7
1. Cacti—Southwest, New—Identification. 2. Cactus—Southwest, New—Pictorial works. I. Title

QK495.C11 Q56 2001   2001006282
583'.56'0979—dc21

Printed in Korea
10 9 8 7 6 5 4 3 2

INTRODUCTION

Cacti are a fascinating family of plants with many unusual forms, a wide range of sizes, and often stunningly beautiful flowers. Although they occur in a variety of habitats, cacti are a common feature of deserts and are uniquely adapted to conditions of extreme heat and drought. All but one species of cacti are native to the New World and the family is widely distributed, ranging as far north as Canada and as far south as Argentina. Indigenous peoples of the Americas have long used cacti for food, wine, dyes, medicine, religious ceremonies, building and fencing material, fish poison, fishhooks, firewood, furniture, and tools.

Sixteenth century Europeans regarded cacti as horticultural oddities and began to propagate them. Today, cacti are grown as prized specimens in private and public collections around the globe. Where the climate is favorable, many cacti have found their way into desert gardens as drought-tolerant accents.

Cacti are only one of several plant families that exhibit succulence—the ability to store water in leaves, stems, or roots. This capacity for water storage is an adaptation that evolved primarily as a response to arid environments. Many unrelated succulent plants, such as agave and ocotillo, are often mistakenly assumed to be cacti. Some African succulents, including euphorbias, bear a remarkable resemblance to cacti, but they too are unrelated and have simply evolved similar adaptations to their environment. To identify specific plant families, one must examine the flower and fruiting structures, and other characteristics that determine a plant's taxonomic status.

THE CACTUS FAMILY

Despite the astounding variety of forms, the cactus family is distinguished by a specific set of characteristics. Stem surfaces may be smooth, but typically they have tubercles—structures that are actually enlarged leaf bases. Tubercles may be nipple-like, triangular and leaf-like, or merged into vertical ribs such as those seen on columnar cacti. Some tropical cacti have large leaves, but most species have none. The cholla (*Cylindropuntia*) and prickly pear (*Opuntia*) species produce tiny, ephemeral leaves in spring that are quickly lost.

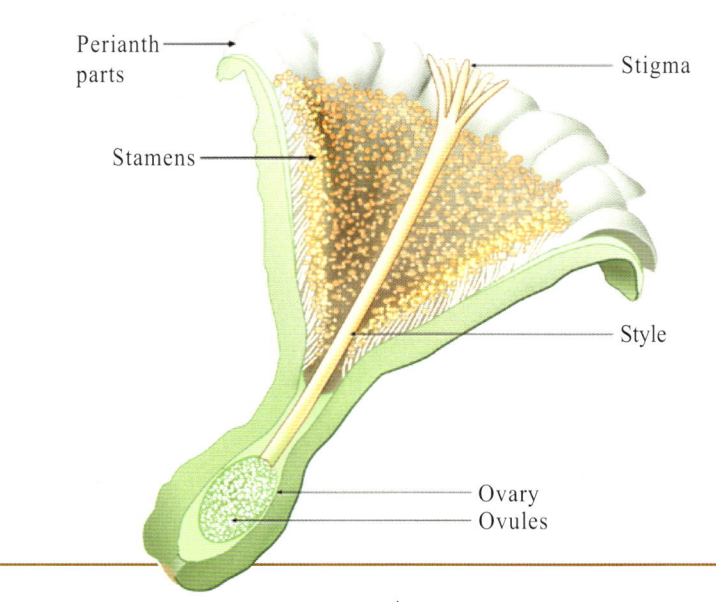

Areoles are specialized structures unique to cacti and consist of small pads or cushions from which spines and flowers emerge in most species. Spines are considered modified leaves; they can be all alike, or the outer radial spines may be distinct from the inner, central spines. Taxonomists often refer to the arrangement, size, and number of spines per areole when describing a species or variety. Spines protect the plants from herbivores, help reduce water loss by slowing air movement, and provide shade. Plant dispersal is aided by the barbed spines on loose cholla joints that catch on to the fur or skin of passing animals. The cholla (*Cylindropuntia*) and prickly pear (*Opuntia*) species have short, often inconspicuous, barbed spines called glochids that easily penetrate the skin and are difficult to remove.

Many cactus flowers are surprising in their beauty, size, and brilliance of color. The flowers do not have distinct sepals and petals. Instead, the flower parts are more green and sepal-like on the outer edge of the flower and more colorful and petal-like toward the center and inner edges. These perianth parts (petals and sepals collectively) are united at their bases into a floral tube. This tube arises from the ovary at the base of the flower. Bees are the primary pollinators of most cacti, though some genera are adapted for pollination by birds, bats, butterflies, or moths. Flower color, shape, fragrance and time of opening are all factors that influence the evolution of specific plant-pollinator relationships. Following pollination and fertilization, the ovules develop into seeds and the ovary swells to become the fruit. Most frequently, birds consume the fruits and disperse seeds by passing them in their droppings. Ants, reptiles, and mammals also disperse fruits of some species.

SOUTHWEST DESERTS

The Mojave Desert is the smallest and driest of the North American deserts. It is centered in southern California and includes small areas of southern Nevada, southwestern Utah, and northwestern Arizona. Average annual rainfall is two to ten inches, falling mainly in winter and spring. Winters are cold and snow often dusts the ground. Vegetation consists of low shrubs, grasses, cacti, yuccas, and wildflowers. The arborescent Joshua tree (*Yucca brevifolia*) dominates the landscape at elevations above 3,000 feet and roughly delineates the boundary of this desert. There are about twenty-five species of cacti, primarily prickly pear (*Opuntia*) and cholla *(Cylindropuntia)* species. Elevations range from below sea level to 4,000 feet.

The Chihuahuan Desert lies mainly in the Mexican state of Chihuahua but also includes portions of Durango, Zacatecas, Nuevo Leon, and Sonora. In the United States, this desert extends up into southwestern Texas, New Mexico, and southeastern Arizona. A warm, temperate desert in the north, it becomes subtropical toward the southern limits. Elevations range from 1,000 to 6,000 feet and

Boise
OREGON
IDAHO
WYOMING
GREAT
BASIN
DESERT
Reno
NEVADA
Salt Lake City
UTAH
WASATCH MTNS
Green
River
ROCKY
MOUNTAINS
Denver
COLORADO
Moab
CALIFORNIA
St. George
COLORADO
PLATEAU
Durango
Las
Vegas
MOJAVE
DESERT
River
SANGRE DE CHRISTO
MTNS
Hualapai
Havasupai
Little
Colorado
River
Hopi
Navajo
Santa Fe
Los
Angeles
Palm
Springs
Colorado
Flagstaff
Albuquerque
Yavapai
ARIZONA
Cahuilla
WHITE MTNS
Grande
San
Diego
River Yuman
Phoenix
Salt R.
Western
Apache
NEW MEXICO
Gila
River
Maricopa
Pima
MOGOLLON
MTNS
Rio
SONORAN
DESERT
Tucson
San Pedro
Chiricahua
Apache
O'odham
BAJA
CALIFORNIA
NORTE
Nogales
UNITED STATES
MEXICO
El Paso
Ciudad
Juárez
TEXAS
SIERRA MADRE
N
Seri
SONORA
Yaqui
Rio Sonora
CHIHUAHUA
Hermosillo
Chihuahua
CHIHUAHUAN
DESERT
Rio
Yaqui
Rio Conchos
BAJA
CALIFORNIA
SUR
COAHUILA
Pacific
Ocean
SINALOA
DURANGO
© Paul Mirocha

characteristic vegetation includes small shrubs, leaf succulents, and numerous species of cacti. Lechuguilla *(Agave lechuguilla)* is a dominant species throughout a large portion of this desert. Rainfall averages about ten inches annually and falls mainly in summer, with some winter rain occurring in the northernmost region. More than three hundred species of cacti are found in the Chihuahuan Desert.

The Sonoran Desert, with its distinctive legume trees and columnar cacti, is characterized by a bi-seasonal rainfall pattern and mild winters. The notable variety of life forms also includes many small cacti, leaf succulents, shrubs, and perennial and annual wildflowers. The Sonoran Desert encompasses large portions of the Mexican states of Sonora, Baja California Norte, and Baja California Sur, as well as southern Arizona and southeastern California in the U.S. Elevations range from below sea level to 3,500 feet. Rainfall ranges from about two to fifteen inches and will vary considerably in the different regions, and from year to year. Gentle winter rains sweep in from the Pacific Ocean and are widespread, thoroughly soaking large areas. Summer thunderstorms originating in the gulfs of Mexico and California are often localized and can dump large amounts of rain in a short period. About one hundred species of cacti occur in the Sonoran Desert region.

CLASSIFICATION OF CACTI

Cacti in this book are presented alphabetically by botanical name. The botanical names and classification system used in this guide are based on those published in *The Cactus Family* by Edward Anderson, published in 2001. Anderson based his system on that developed by the International Cactaceae Systematics Group of the International Organization for Succulent Plant Study (IOS). This group of specialists has been working since 1984 to sort out the complex issues associated with the classification and naming of cacti.

We also have attempted to identify each species in this book by its most widely accepted common name, or names, but these are less precise and can be confusing. In many cases, a particular species may be known by several common names (e.g. Turk's head, eagle claw, blue barrel), and many species share the same or similar common name (e.g. strawberry hedgehog and strawberry cactus).

CONSERVATION

Many cacti have been adversely affected by human activities, including habitat destruction and illegal collection from the wild. In extreme cases, entire populations of some species have been lost and others have been significantly reduced.

For example, urban development in the Southwest has severely impacted magnificent stands of irreplaceable saguaros. In Mexico, the conversion of marginal land to agriculture and ranching has destroyed or damaged large populations of cacti. Introduced animals, especially goats, have had a devastating affect on cacti in many localities. And, illegal collection of huge numbers of rare cacti by individuals who sell plants to collectors has also depleted natural populations.

Collectors and hobbyists who understand the need to preserve these plants in the wild willingly purchase only propagated plants from reputable nurseries. These nurseries should be encouraged to propagate rare species, as their efforts help to satisfy the demand for the plants, while taking pressure off wild populations. Legally conducted salvage operations can help save many cacti from destruction in areas where development is inevitable. The long-term survival rate for mature specimens of transplanted cacti, however, is discouragingly low for some species.

The issues of habitat preservation and protection of rare species continue to prove challenging in the face of increasing human pressures. Scientists, hobbyists, hikers, and concerned citizens are conducting valuable research and conservation efforts in many areas. Readers are encouraged to join their local cactus and succulent clubs, native plant societies, botanical gardens, and conservation organizations to learn more about the issues in their region, and to find out how to lend their support.

LIVING ROCK CACTUS
Ariocarpus fissuratus

Often growing flush with the soil surface, the living rock cactus is so flat and inconspicuous that one may step on it, unaware. Once seen, the star-shaped pattern of the tubercles is unmistakable. The fleshy, subterranean stem—three to five inches diameter—is topped with spineless, flattened and highly textured tubercles. Showy clusters of brilliant pink flowers emerge from the center of the plant in the fall. The small, oblong fruits remain embedded in the wool until they disintegrate and release the seeds. Living rock cactus is typically found in limestone soils with rock fragments. All six species of *Ariocarpus* occur in the Chihuahuan Desert; only *A. fissuratus* is found in the U.S. and is common in the Big Bend region of Texas. Sometimes called false peyote or sunami, *A. fissuratus* has been used by the Tarahumara to make an intoxicating, ceremonial drink.

Elevation: 1,500–4,000 feet

Range: West Texas; Chihuahua and Coahuila, Mexico

SAND DOLLAR (Sea Urchin Cactus)
Astrophytum asterias

This round, flattened cactus features prominent areoles but is virtually free of spines. Distinct lines and delicate white spotting form a pattern that resembles a sea urchin. Bright yellow, two-inch-wide flowers with red bases, which emerge at the top center of the plant, bloom intermittently in the summer months. These are followed by thin-walled fruits that are clothed in a layer of white woolly hairs.

Sand dollar occurs primarily in thornscrub vegetation in south Texas, and Nuevo Leon and Tamaulipas, Mexico. The range of this species has been severely reduced due to collecting and habitat destruction, and the U.S. Fish and Wildlife Service list this cactus as endangered. There are only four species within the genus *Astrophytum*; *A. asterias* is the only one found within U.S. borders. All four are popular among hobbyists and widely grown in nurseries and cactus collections.

Elevation: 300–1,000 feet

Range: South Texas; Nuevo Leon and Tamaulipas, Mexico

GOLDEN TORCH (Velvet Cactus)
Bergerocactus emoryi

Covered with masses of bristly golden spines, golden torch is a handsome columnar cactus with erect or trailing stems growing to seven feet high and forming dense colonies. Blooming April through May, the pale yellow flowers appear at the branch tips and are followed by spiny, red, globose fruits that dry at maturity. Golden torch typically occurs in sandy soils on bluffs and in arroyos of coastal chaparral vegetation in southern California and northern Baja. XPacherocactus is a rare, naturally occurring inter-generic hybrid between *Pachycereus pringlei* and *Bergerocactus emoryi*. It is known only from a few localities in Baja California, Mexico.

Elevation: Sea level–200 feet

Range: Southern California and some of the Channel Islands; northwestern Baja California, Mexico

SAGUARO
Carnegiea gigantea

A dramatic and fitting symbol of the Sonoran Desert, the massive saguaro cactus is an unmistakable, large columnar plant with upright arms that branch from a single main trunk. The treelike plants can grow to a height of fifty-two feet, and mature specimens are estimated to be up to 250 years of age. Ribs number 12–30. The large, funnel-shaped, sturdy white flowers occur in clusters on and around the stem tips, and can be up to five inches long. Saguaro flowers bloom in late spring and are pollinated by birds, bees, and nectar-feeding bats. The oblong, nearly spineless, greenish to pinkish fruits ripen in early summer. The fruits eventually burst open, revealing a bright red mass of pulp and seeds that is avidly consumed by desert birds.

Saguaros and their edible fruits have been important to the culture and traditions of the Tohono O'odham, a large tribe that currently inhabits portions of southwestern Arizona and north-western Mexico. Historically, the Tohono O'odham constructed seasonal camps in dense saguaro forests to harvest the abundant fruits. Women collected the fruits with long poles fashioned from the woody ribs of saguaro. They cooked the juice over a fire until it thickened, and then strained out the pulp and seeds to yield a tasty syrup. The consumption of saguaro fruit wine is part of an important ceremony designed to bring bountiful summer rains.

Saguaros occur in rocky or gravelly soils of foothills, canyons and washes.

Elevation: Near sea level–4,500 feet

Range: Southern Arizona, southern California, and Sonora, Mexico

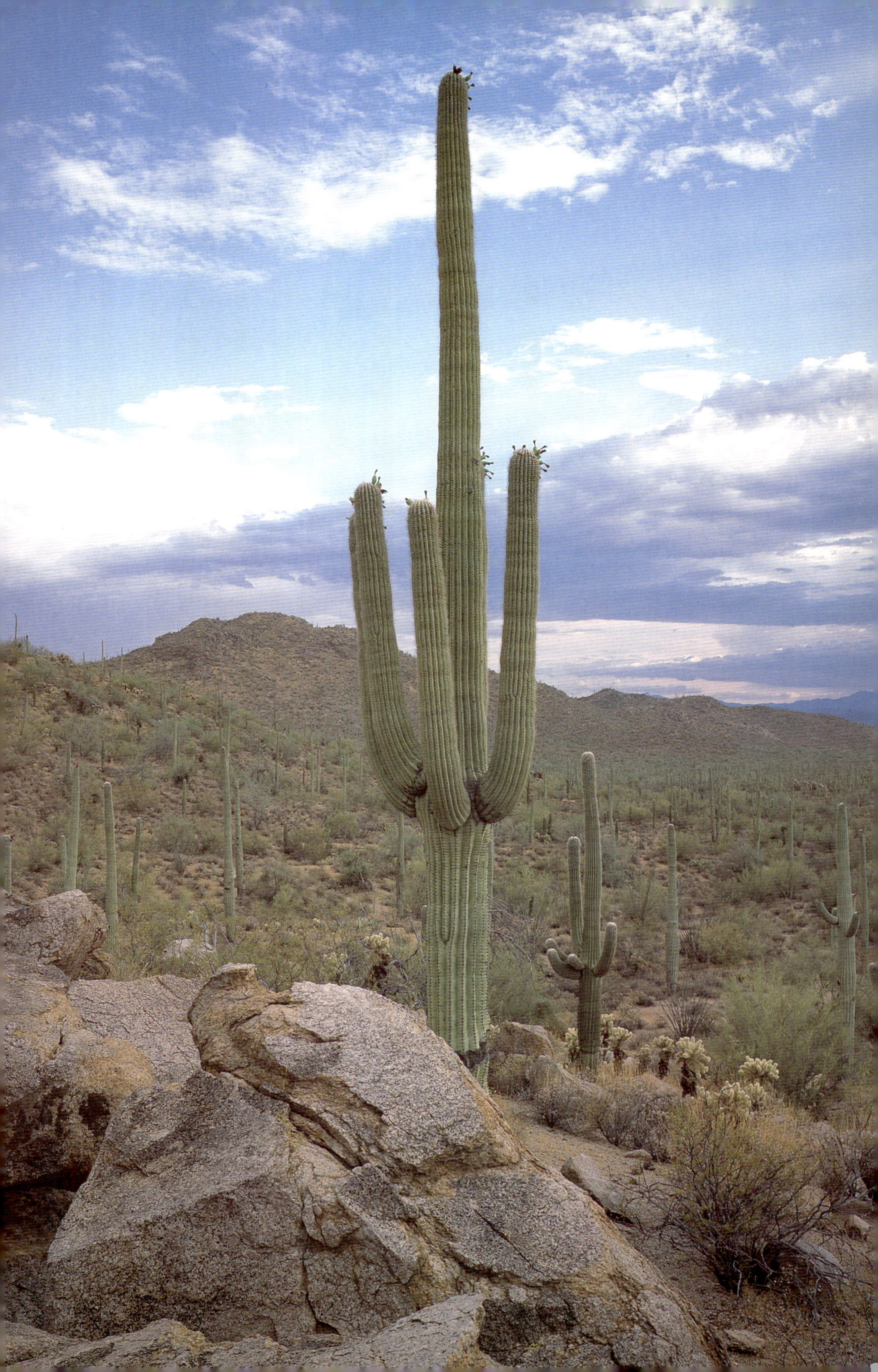

SEA URCHIN CACTUS
Coryphantha echinus

The densely spined, gray-green stems of sea urchin cactus are often solitary but sometimes form large clumps. Gray-green stems can be eight inches high and two and one-half inches in diameter. A one-inch long, upper central spine stands straight out from each spine cluster. Extremely showy, bright yellow flowers with red stamens are born on the stem tips in spring and summer. The emerging fruits remain green, growing to one inch. *C. echinus* is typically found in limestone soils on hillsides of the Chihuahuan Desert and desert grassland. Plants are frequently hidden under shrubs or among grasses.

Elevation: 1,300–4,800 feet

Range: West Texas; Chihuahua and Coahuila, Mexico

ssp. macromeris

LONG MAMMA
Coryphantha macromeris

Solitary or forming dense clumps up to three feet wide, long mamma has conspicuous, elongated tubercles and bright rose-pink flowers, followed by green, fleshy fruits. Widely distributed in the Chihuahuan Desert, it is found in clay or gravelly soils on low hills and flats. Subspecies *macromeris* can have six-inch-high green stems, half-inch tubercles, and is common and widespread in the Chihuahuan Desert. Subspecies *runyonii* is a smaller plant with three-inch-high gray-green stems and shorter tubercles. It occurs only near sea level along the Rio Grande plain.

Elevation: Below 4,500 feet

Range: New Mexico and Texas; Chihuahua, Coahuila, Durango, and Zacatecas, Mexico

SANTA CRUZ BEEHIVE CACTUS
(Golden-Chested Beehive)
Coryphantha recurvata

A stout species with stems to six inches in diameter, Santa Cruz beehive cactus will commonly cluster, forming large mounds with up to fifty stems. Plants are densely covered with golden yellow spines, the central one curving downward. One-inch-wide, pale yellow flowers emerge in a ring around the stem tips in summer and develop into fruits that are green, round, and fleshy at maturity. Santa Cruz beehive cactus is found in grassland and oak woodland habitats, growing in a sunny exposure or sheltered by trees and shrubs.

Elevation: 4,000–6,000 feet

Range: Southern Arizona and Sonora, Mexico

PINEAPPLE CACTUS
(Pima Pineapple Cactus)
Coryphantha robustispina

These globose plants are solitary or clumping, growing six to twelve inches tall with gray-green stems to three and a half inches in diameter, and stout, tubercles. Spines are white to gray with dark tips; the one to four central spines can be straight, curved or hooked. Flowers range from dark golden yellow to a pale yellow followed by cylindrical, two-inch-long green fruits.

Subspecies *robustispina* is found mainly in southern Arizona and is listed as endangered by the U.S. Fish and Wildlife Service under the name *C. scheeri* ssp. *robustispina*. It has a single, curved or hooked, stout central spine and occurs in desert grassland or woodland, at elevations of 2,300–5,000 feet. *C. robustispina* ssp. *scheeri* has straight central spines and occurs on sandy flats below 4,000 feet in west Texas, New Mexico, and Chihuahua, Mexico. *C. robustispina* ssp. *uncinata* has strongly curved or hooked central spines and typically grows on rocky hillsides below 4,000 feet in Arizona, New Mexico, west Texas, and Chihuahua.

Elevation: 2,300–5,000 feet, depending on subspecies

Range: Southern Arizona, New Mexico, and Texas; Sonora and Chihuahua, Mexico

ssp. robustispina

BUCKHORN CHOLLA
Cylindropuntia acanthocarpa

Buckhorn is a many-branched, shrubby or tree-like cholla growing four to six feet high. When present, the main trunk is short—less than one fifth the height of the plant. The two-inch-wide, brightly colored flowers are highly variable, ranging from amber to orange to dark red. Fruits are dry, tan, and very spiny at maturity. These spiny fruits are a reliable characteristic to look for when trying to distinguish buckhorn from staghorn cholla. Buckhorn cholla tends to be shrubby in central and eastern Arizona and more tree-like in southern California. In times of cold or drought, the plant will turn a striking reddish or purplish color.

Flower buds of *C. acanthocarpa* served as an important staple food for Native Americans of the Sonoran desert region, including the Apache, River Pima, and Tohono O'odham. Typically, buds were gathered using tongs, and spines were removed either before or after cooking. Large roasting pits, lined with rocks, were used for steaming the buds for about twelve hours. Once cooked, the buds could be dried and stored indefinitely to provide year-round sustenance. Nutritional studies have shown that cholla buds contain high amounts of calcium and moderate amounts of iron.

Elevation: 300–4,000 feet

Range: Southern California, southern Nevada, southwestern Utah, and southern Arizona

PENCIL CHOLLA
Cylindropuntia arbuscula

Pencil cholla is a densely branching shrub or dwarf tree with slightly larger than pencil-diameter stems and few spines. Plants range from two to ten feet in height. Tubercles are generally narrow and inconspicuous. In late spring, yellow to bronze flowers emerge on stem tips, followed by fleshy, spineless fruits that are green to pale yellow. Pencil cholla is a Sonoran Desert species found in sandy and gravelly soils of flats, washes or valleys. The River Pima sometimes gathered the flower buds of inferior-tasting *C. arbuscula*, especially if the harvest of *C. acanthocarpa* was poor. The fleshy, spineless fruits of *C. arbuscula* also have been used for food, raw or cooked.

Elevation: 1,000–3,000 feet

Range: Southern Arizona; Sonora, Mexico

TEDDY BEAR CHOLLA
Cylindropuntia bigelovii

Teddy bear is a shrubby, densely spined cholla with upright stems and dark trunks. Specimens can grow to about six and a half feet tall, although most are considerably shorter. Interlacing golden spines are so thick that they obscure the body of the plant. Loose joints drop readily, and the strongly barbed spines attach easily to passing animals, which serve as unwitting dispersal agents. Teddy bear, like many chollas, relies primarily on vegetative reproduction and produces few viable seeds. On dry, steep slopes where it is typically seen, extensive colonies of a single clone will form where joints have fallen and taken root. Pale, greenish-white flowers appear in the spring, followed by leathery fruits with prominent tubercles. Teddy bear cholla is widespread in the Sonoran and Mojave deserts.

var. bigelovii

Variety *bigelovii* is common throughout the range. Variety *ciribe* occurs only in southern Baja and tends to produce long chains of fruit. The Cahuilla collected and pit-baked the flower buds of teddy bear cholla. The Seri cooked and ate the young joints after burning off the spines.

Elevation: 100–3,500 feet

Range: Southern California and western and southern Arizona; Sonora and Baja California, Mexico

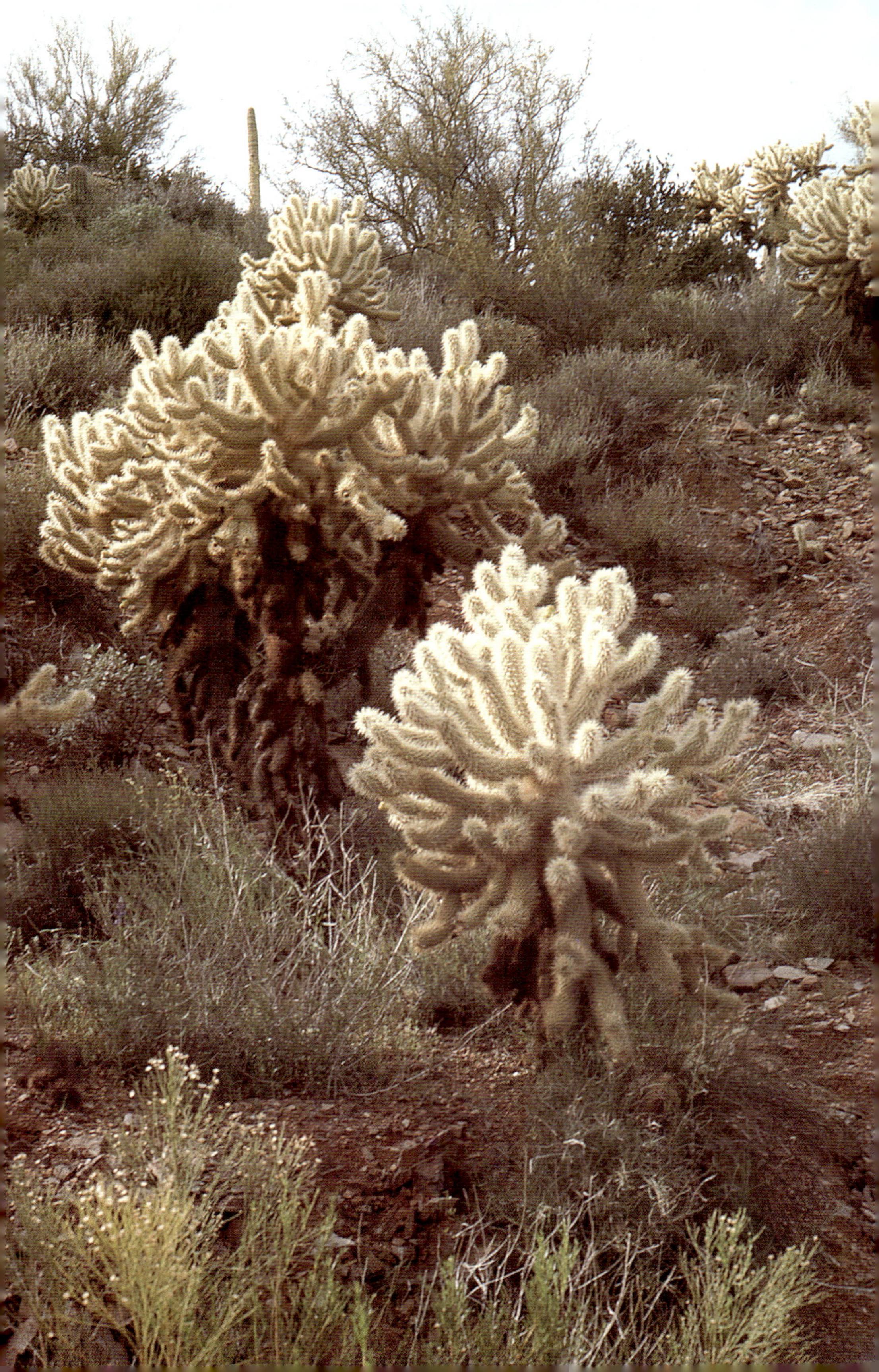

SILVER or GOLD CHOLLA
Cylindropuntia echinocarpa

The dense spines of *Cylindropuntia echinocarpa* can be either white or yellow and will strongly affect the overall color of the plant, hence the name of silver or gold cholla. Plants are quite shrubby and grow to a height of one to six feet. Two-inch-wide, greenish-yellow flowers are followed by dry, spiny, light tan or straw-colored fruits. Silver or gold cholla is found on sandy or gravelly soils of benches, slopes, and flats primarily in Mojave Desert localities. The fruits were rolled on the ground to remove the spines and eaten raw by the Maricopa, Mojave, and Cocopa.

Elevation: 1,000–5,000 feet

Range: Southern California, Nevada, Utah, and western Arizona

CHAIN-FRUIT or JUMPING CHOLLA
Cylindropuntia fulgida

A large, treelike species with branching crowns and wide, spreading trunks, the chain fruit cholla at maturity can be fifteen feet tall and is covered with dense, light yellow spines. On mature plants the supporting trunks turn very dark. The light colored joints detach easily, barbed spines hooking tenaciously onto unsuspecting passers-by. Pink to magenta flowers open in the late afternoon and are followed by spineless, fleshy green fruits that persist for years, forming long chains. Chain-fruit cholla grows best in sandy soils of low bajadas and valleys and is common throughout the Sonoran Desert. It often forms extensive dense forests where loose joints have fallen and taken root.

var. fulgida

Two varieties are often recognized. *C. fulgida* var. *fulgida* is the common form with one-and-one-half-inch spines, six to twelve per areole. *C. fulgida* var. *mamillata* has spines less than an inch in length, two to six per areole. *C. fulgida* var. *mamillata* also has a lower and denser growth form, very prominent tubercles, and inconspicuous spines.

The abundant, fleshy fruits of chain-fruit cholla were frequently harvested and eaten by the Seri. Fruits were gathered at any time of year and eaten fresh, boiled and mashed with honey, or briefly roasted in hot coals.

Elevation: 1,000–3,000 feet

Range: Widely distributed throughout the Sonoran Desert and Sinaloa, Mexico

var. imbricata

TREE CHOLLA
Cylindropuntia imbricata

Tree cholla is a small tree or thicket-forming shrub growing three to ten feet high, with a short trunk and long branches, and exceedingly prominent tubercles. During cold or drought the branches will often turn a striking shade of purple. The one-inch wide, deep pink to magenta flowers are followed by strongly tuberculate, spineless fruits that ripen to a bright lemon yellow. Tree cholla occurs on gravelly or sandy soils of hills, plains and washes in grassland.

Two varieties are recognized. Variety *imbricata* is treelike, growing to ten feet high, with small stem segments. Variety *argentea* is shrubby with large stem segments, and occurs only in the Big Bend region of Texas.

Fruits of tree cholla were gathered, pit baked, dried, and stored by the Pima, and were eaten raw or cooked by the White Mountain Apache. Stem joints were cooked and eaten by people of the Laguna and Acoma pueblos.

Elevation: 2,000–6,000 feet

Range: Eastern Arizona, Colorado, New Mexico, and Texas; Chihuahua and Coahuila, Mexico.

CHRISTMAS CHOLLA
Cylindropuntia leptocaulis

Christmas cholla is the most slender of all chollas, with stems measuring often less than a quarter inch in diameter. Each areole bears only one down-turned spine and numerous glochids. Greenish, yellow, or bronze flowers emerge in summer and develop into bright red, grape-sized fruits that persist through the winter months.

Christmas cholla is found growing under the protection of trees or shrubs in a variety of habitats including deserts, grasslands, chaparral, and woodland.

Though small, the fruits of Christmas cholla are edible and tasty, and were consumed as a ready-to-eat food by many Southwest tribes.

Elevation: 200–5,000 feet

Range: Widely distributed throughout the southwestern U.S. and northern Mexico

COASTAL CHOLLA
Cylindropuntia prolifera

A shrubby or treelike plant that grows six to eight feet tall, coastal cholla is gray-green with easily detachable joints, each three to six inches long. The needle-like spines are reddish brown to dark brown, a half to one inch in length. In late spring and early summer, bright rose to magenta flowers emerge on stem tips, followed by fleshy and typically sterile fruits, which form short chains of two to five segments. This species reproduces primarily vegetatively—both joints and fruits will take root and produce new plants. Coastal cholla occurs on ocean bluffs and coastal hills, and often forms dense thickets.

Elevation: Sea level–300 feet

Range: Southern California and Baja California, Mexico

DIAMOND CHOLLA
Cylindropuntia ramosissima

A narrow-stemmed, shrubby or treelike species, diamond cholla can grow from eighteen inches to six and a half feet in height. The grayish stems have diamond-shaped, grooved tubercles and two-inch-long, needlelike spines, although some populations are spineless. Bronze-red flowers are followed by tan, burr-like fruits. Diamond cholla is found in fine or sandy soils of washes and desert flats, and is widespread in the Mojave and Sonoran deserts. It grows to its largest size, six and a half feet, on the western edge of the Mojave Desert. Otherwise, it tends to be shrubby and rarely more than thirty inches tall.

Elevation: 100–3,000 feet

Range: Arizona, California, and Nevada, and Baja California

CANE CHOLLA

Cylindropuntia spinosior

This treelike, frost-hardy cholla can grow to eight feet high with single or multiple trunks. The two-inch-wide flowers are commonly reddish-purple and are followed by lemon-yellow fleshy fruits. Cane cholla is found primarily in grassland habitats, but also occurs in chaparral, woodland and montane forests. Plants growing in New Mexico will intergrade with *C. imbricata*. Hybrids occur between *C. spinosior* and *C. versicolor*, especially in the eastern range of *C. versicolor*.

The Tohono O'odham, River Pima, and Apache gathered, cooked, and ate the fruits and seeds of cane cholla.

Elevation: 2,000–6,500 feet

Range: Southern Arizona and New Mexico, and Sonora and Chihuahua, Mexico

STAGHORN CHOLLA
Cylindropuntia versicolor

Generally treelike though sometimes shrubby, staghorn cholla grows to about seven feet high with stout, gray trunks. Entire plants will turn purple in times of cold or drought. Flowers are richly colored and variable, occurring in dark red, lavender, magenta, amber, or brown. Fruits are generally spineless and green, with tinges of purple color and often form short chains of two or three fruits. Immature fruits often have spines that detach as the fruits ripen. Staghorn cholla is found in sandy soils of canyons, washes, and valleys. It is most abundant on the Tohono O'odham reservation near Tucson. The fleshy fruits of staghorn cholla were occasionally collected by the Tohono O'odham and Pima and pit-baked, although flower buds were much preferred.

Elevation: 2,000–3,000 feet

Range: Southern Arizona and Sonora, Mexico

var. horizonthalonius

TURK'S HEAD CACTUS
(Eagle Claw, Blue Barrel)
Echinocactus horizonthalonius

Growing to about softball-size, Turk's head cactus is usually solitary but occasionally will form small clumps. The body of the plant is an attractive blue-green color with distinct ribs, usually eight, lined with spine clusters that are gray or reddish. Brilliant pink flowers emerge in a cluster at the stem tips in late spring and summer. The one-inch-long fruits are covered with dense, woolly hairs and eventually fall off as the stem grows, dropping the seeds at the base of the plant. Variety *horizonthalonius* is common in limestone soils on rocky hills throughout a broad area of the Chihuahuan Desert. It does not cluster and rarely grows higher than ten inches. Variety *nicholii* is listed as endangered by the U.S. Fish and Wildlife Service. It is rare in southern Arizona and northwestern Sonora, Mexico.

Elevation: 1,300–5,500 feet

Range: Southern Arizona, New Mexico, and Texas south to San Luis Potosi, Mexico

MANY-HEADED BARREL
Echinocactus polycephalus

Many-headed barrel will branch to form magnificent mounds three to five feet in diameter, with as many as one hundred heads. Dense, whitish-gray and felty spines often obscure the body of the plant. Light yellow flowers with pink midribs open in midsummer. These develop into one-inch-long fruits that are densely covered with white woolly hairs and are dry at maturity. Subspecies *polycephalus* is most widespread, forms large mounds, and is common on rocky slopes in arid regions of the Mojave and Sonoran deserts below 2,500 feet. Subspecies *xeranthemoides* forms smaller clumps and is found in pinyon-juniper woodland at 3,300 to 4,900 feet in northern Arizona, southern Nevada, and southern Utah

Native Americans have used spines of many-headed barrel as fishhooks and as awls in basketmaking.

Elevation: 100–5,000 feet

Range: California, Arizona, Nevada, and Utah, and northwestern Sonora, Mexico

ssp. polycephalus

HORSE CRIPPLER
Echinocactus texensis

This solitary cactus grows to about a foot in diameter and eight inches tall. The stout, tapering, cross-striated spines are indeed dangerous to horses and humans. The single central spine is down-curved and flattened. Plants often grow close to the soil surface where they are not immediately evident to unwary travelers. Flowers are showy, up to two and one half inches wide and range from white to pale pink or deep pink with red centers. The walnut-size fruits are bright red and fleshy at maturity. Horse crippler is common on limestone or sandy soils of hillsides and valleys in the Chihuahuan Desert and adjacent grassland, thornscrub, and woodland habitats.

Elevation: Sea level–3,300 feet

Range: Southeastern New Mexico, southwestern Oklahoma, and Texas, and Coahuila, Nuevo Leon, and Tamaulipas, Mexico

Bonker Hedgehog
Echinocereus bonkerae (E. engelmannii *var.* bonkerae)

One of the most handsome of all hedgehogs, Bonker hedgehog forms compact clumps of five to fifteen stems, has short spines, and extremely large, showy flowers. Lavish, deep magenta to purple blooms occur on the upper stems in spring and can be up to four inches wide. Fruits are fleshy and plump, ripening to a bright red color. Bonker hedgehog is found in desert grasslands, on hillsides, and in canyons in Sonoran Desert localities.

Elevation: 3,000–6,000 feet

Range: Central and southern Arizona, Sonora, Mexico

CHISOS MOUNTAIN HEDGEHOG
Echinocereus chisoensis

Two distinct varieties of chisos mountain hedgehog are recognized. *E. chisoensis* var. *chisoensis* occurs in the limestone flats and hillsides of west Texas in Big Bend National Park below 3,300 feet. It has become quite rare due to illegal collecting and is listed as threatened by the U.S. Fish and Wildlife Service. It has cylindrical stems and whitish spines, and grows to a height of about ten inches. The flowers are extremely large and showy, up to three inches wide, bright pink at the outer edges, white in the middle, and deep red at the base. *E. chisoensis* var. *fobeanus* has stems that are constricted into annual sections, with flowers almost four inches long. It occurs above 3,300 feet in Durango and Coahuila, Mexico.

Elevation: 2,000–4,000 feet

Range: West Texas, and Durango and Coahuila, Mexico

var. chisoensis

TEXAS RAINBOW
Echinocereus dasyacanthus (E. pectinatus var. dasyacanthus)

The mostly solitary stems of Texas rainbow are cylindrical and tapering at the tips, growing to fourteen inches high. Interlacing spines—ranging from yellow to pink to brown—are short and dense and obscure the body of the plant. Lemon yellow flowers up to six inches wide arise from the sides of the stems. Flowers can also be whitish, orange, pink, or purple. Fruits are fleshy and round, green to purple, with deciduous spines. Texas rainbow is found on limestone hills and flats in desert grassland and Chihuahuan desert scrub.

Elevation: 2,000–5,000 feet

Range: New Mexico and west Texas; Chihuahua and Coahuila, Mexico

ENGELMANN'S HEDGEHOG
(Strawberry Hedgehog)
Echinocereus engelmannii

Engelmann's hedgehog forms open or compact clumps up to three and a half feet wide. The stout and formidable spines are variable in color and size and can be up to three inches long. Funnel-shaped, spring-blooming flowers are born on the upper stems, ranging in color from purple to bright pink to lavender, with deep green stigmas. Nine varieties have been recognized. The edible fruits of Engelmann's hedgehog are scarlet-red, juicy, and sweet. Spines fall from the mature fruits, making them easy to harvest and consume. They were seasonally used as a food by the Pima, Tohono O'odham, and other southwestern tribes.

Elevation: Sea level–7,900 feet

Range: Widely distributed in the southwestern U.S. and northwestern Mexico

STRAWBERRY HEDGEHOG
Echinocereus enneacanthus

A profusely branching species, strawberry hedgehog will form large clumps with up to two hundred stems. Stems can grow to a foot tall and four inches in diameter. Deep pink to magenta flowers arise below the stem tips followed by purplish, round to oval, edible fruits that have a taste similar to strawberries.

Subspecies *enneacanthus* has stems two to six inches in diameter, long and curved central spines, and one-and-a-half-inch radials. It is common on limestone and clay-loam soils on rocky hills, washes, and plains in grassland or desert. Subspecies *brevispinus* has narrower stems, erect and straight central spines, and shorter radials. It occurs in south Texas and northern Mexico below 3,000 feet on gravelly soils in grassland and desert.

Elevation: Sea level–4,000 feet

Range: Texas, New Mexico and northern Mexico

ssp. enneacanthus

ROBUST HEDGEHOG
Echinocereus fasciculatus

Robust hedgehog occurs in loose clumps of five to twenty cylindrical stems up to eighteen inches tall. The principal central spines, one to three inches long, are light colored with dark tips, which is characteristic of this species. Broad, funnel shaped, magenta to reddish purple flowers occur on the upper stems. Fruits are round and fleshy, and turn red when ripe. Robust hedgehog is found on sandy and rocky hillsides and washes in the Sonoran Desert and adjacent grasslands. Two hedgehogs formerly listed as varieties of this species–*bonkerae* and *boyce-thompsonii*–are now accepted as separate species.

Elevation: 2,000–5,000 feet

Range: Arizona and New Mexico; Sonora, Mexico

FENDLER'S HEDGEHOG
Echinocereus fendleri

Fendler's hedgehog is a single- or multiple-stemmed plant that sometimes forms loose clumps with as many as ten stems growing to ten inches tall. One very dark central spine is usually present, straight or curving slightly; radials are white. Deep magenta, funnel-shaped flowers arise on the upper stems followed by round, red, fleshy, and edible fruits. This species is found in grasslands and oak or juniper woodland.

Three subspecies are recognized. Subspecies *fendleri*, which has one curved central spine, is typically solitary or with few stems, and is found above 5,900 feet. Subspecies *hempelii* has no central spines and is found only in Mexico. Subspecies *rectispinus* may have up to ten stems, one straight central spine (sometimes absent), and occurs below 5,400 feet. *E. fendleri* var. *kuenzleri* is listed as endangered by the U.S. Fish and Wildlife Service, although its taxonomic status is uncertain.

Elevation: 3,000–8,000 feet

Range: Arizona, New Mexico, Colorado, and Texas; Chihuahua and Sonora, Mexico

ssp. rectispinus

LEDING'S HEDGEHOG
Echinocereus ledingii

Known only from the mountains of southeastern Arizona, Leding's hedgehog forms clumps of four to ten stems up to about a foot in height. Striking yellowish or straw-colored spines give the whole plant a golden hue. Large and showy flowers, ranging from rosy-pink to purple, are born in late spring near the stem tips, followed by round, red, fleshy, and edible fruits. This species is found on rocky or gravelly mountain slopes, in grassland, and oak woodland.

Elevation: 4,000–6,000 feet

Range: Southeastern Arizona

MOJAVE HEDGEHOG
Echinocereus mojavensis (E. triglochidiatus *var.* mojavensis)

These plants can form impressive mounds with as many as five hundred stems. A single, two-inch-long central spine is present. Radial spines are often curving and twisted. Striking, orange-red flowers with rounded petaloid tips and lime green stigmas bloom in late spring and are pollinated by hummingbirds. The flowers are followed by one-inch, oblong fruits. Mojave hedgehog is found on rocky hillsides and canyons of the Mojave Desert, coastal chaparral, and pinyon-juniper woodland. This species was formerly considered a variety of *E. triglochidiatus*.

Elevation: 3,500–8,000 feet

Range: Southern California, southern Nevada, southwestern Utah, and northwestern Arizona; northeastern Baja California, Mexico

GOLDEN HEDGEHOG
Echinocereus nicholii (E. engelmannii *var.* nicholii)

Golden hedgehog will form large loose clumps with up to 30 erect, cylindrical stems growing to three feet tall. The spines are very dense and exceptionally striking—golden yellow or white and up to two and a half inches long. Pale lavender to pink flowers emerge on the upper stems, followed by oval fruits that turn red at maturity. The lavender to pink flowering subspecies *nicholii* occurs in southern Arizona and northern Sonora on gravelly or sandy desert flats. Subspecies *llanuraensis* produces crimson flowers and fruits that do not split open and is found only in the vicinity of Guaymas, Sonora. The Pima consumed the fruits of *E. nicholii* ssp. *nicholii* as a ready-to-eat food.

Elevation: 100–3,000 feet

Range: Southern Arizona and northern Sonora, Mexico

ssp. nicholii

ARIZONA RAINBOW
Echinocereus rigidissimus (E. pectinatus *var.* rigidissimus)

Usually a single-stemmed plant, the Arizona rainbow grows up to a foot tall with stems to four and a half inches in diameter. The stems are often obscured by short, dense, interlacing radial spines, which form bands of red, white, yellow, or brown and give the impression of a rainbow. Blossoms of Arizona rainbow are large and showy—up to three and a half inches wide and brilliant pink to purple with a white throat. Fruits are oval, green to red, and heavily spined.

Arizona rainbow is typically found in grassland and oak woodland. Two subspecies are recognized. Subspecies *rigidissimus* has stems to four and a half inches in diameter and occurs in Arizona, New Mexico, and Sonora, Mexico. Subspecies *rubrispinus* has stems to only two and a half inches in diameter and occurs only in Chihuahua, Mexico.

Elevation: 4,000–5,500 feet

Range: Southwestern U.S. and northwestern Mexico

ssp. rigidissimus

STRAWBERRY CACTUS
(Spiny Strawberry Hedgehog)
Echinocereus stramineus

The strawberry cactus forms huge, impressive mounds three and a half to five feet wide and about eighteen inches high, with as many as five hundred stems. When not in bloom, these plants can be recognized by their extremely long and dense, straw-colored spines. Large, magnificent flowers are a rich magenta color and up to five inches wide, followed by juicy, red fruits that smell and taste like strawberries. Strawberry cactus is common on limestone hills of west Texas, and Nuevo Leon and Coahuila, Mexico. Subspecies *stramineus* is widespread throughout the range of the species. Subspecies *occidentalis* occurs only in Durango, Mexico, and blooms at least a month later than subspecies *stramineus*.

Elevation: 2,000–5,000 feet

Range: Southern New Mexico, and west Texas; north central Mexico

ssp. stramineus

CLARET CUP CACTUS
Echinocereus triglochidiatus (E. coccineus)

This cactus will branch profusely, forming mounds to three to five feet wide with up to five hundred stems. Central spines of claret cup cactus are often indistinguishable from the radials. The brilliant flowers—orange-red to dark red with whitish throats, or solid red—remain open for several days and are pollinated by hummingbirds. Fruits are round to oval in shape, turning pink or red at maturity. This cactus occurs in a broad range of elevations and in a variety of habitats, including desert, grassland, woodland and montane forest. Several varieties of *E. triglochidiatus* have been described but their taxonomic status is unclear.

Elevation: 1,500–10,000 feet

Range: Widely distributed in the southwestern U.S. and northern Mexico

BROWN-FLOWERED HEDGEHOG
(Green-Flowered Hedgehog)
Echinocereus viridiflorus

This widely distributed, cold-hardy species can be found from Wyoming to Texas. The stem, which may be solitary or clumping, grows only to about five inches high, with reddish, cream, or brown colored spines that occur along well-defined ribs. One-inch-wide, green to reddish brown flowers develop into green, pea-sized, densely spined fruits. Brown-flowered hedgehog is found in grasslands and woodlands; five subspecies are recognized. Subspecies *davisii* has small stems with six to nine ribs, is restricted to Brewster County, Texas, and is listed as endangered by the U.S. Fish and Wildlife Service.

Elevation: 2,500–9,000 feet

Range: Wyoming, South Dakota, Colorado, Kansas, New Mexico, Oklahoma, and Texas

ssp. cylindricus

CHIHUAHUA PINEAPPLE CACTUS
Echinomastus intertextus

The egg-shaped, solitary stems of Chihuahua pineapple grow to no more than six inches in height, and are thus easily overlooked in the grassland habitat where it occurs. Spines are dense, somewhat flattened, and pink to gray in color. White to pale pink flowers emerge at the stem tips in early spring, followed by half-inch, dry, greenish fruits.

Elevation: 3,000–5,000 feet

Range: Southeastern Arizona, southern New Mexico, and west Texas; northern Mexico

JOHNSON'S PINEAPPLE CACTUS
Echinomastus johnsoni

These solitary plants can grow to ten inches tall and four inches wide, with a dense covering of reddish spines. The funnel-shaped flowers—each two to three inches wide—emerge in a cluster at the tip of the plant and can be magenta, pink, or greenish yellow. Fruits are tan at maturity and split vertically. Johnson's pineapple cactus is found in granitic soils on hillsides and alluvial fans, primarily in Mojave Desert localities.

Elevation: 1,000–4,000 feet

Range: Eastern California, southern Nevada, and western Arizona

MARIPOSA CACTUS
Echinomastus mariposensis

Stems of the tiny mariposa cactus grow only to about three and a half inches tall and resemble a golf ball in size and shape. The white radial spines are extremely dense, obscuring the stem. Pale pink to white flowers with greenish stigmas emerge in early spring, followed by the half-inch, greenish, globose fruits. Mariposa cactus is known only from the limestone hills of the Big Bend region of Texas and Coahuila, Mexico. It is listed as threatened by the U.S. Fish and Wildlife Service.

Elevation: 2,500–3,000 feet

Range: Big Bend region of west Texas and north central Mexico

WARNOCK CACTUS
Echinomastus warnockii

The single stems of the warnock cactus grow to six inches high, with a covering of dense spines. The four to six central spines are tan with dark tips. Inch-wide, pale pink to white flowers bloom in early spring, followed by small round fruits that are brownish at maturity. Warnock cactus occurs in the limestone hills and gypsum flats of the Chihuahuan Desert.

Elevation: Below 4,000 feet

Range: Big Bend region of west Texas and north central Mexico

BOKE BUTTON CACTUS
Epithelantha bokei

Diminutive and inconspicuous, boke button is similar to the common button (*E. micromeris*), but with narrower and almost always solitary stems one to two inches in diameter. Extremely short, flattened spines give the plant an appealing, touchable appearance. Delicate, white to pale pink, half-inch-wide flowers emerge on the tips of new tubercles at the top center of the plant. Slender, scarlet fruits grow straight up from the slight depression at the stem tip. Boke button occurs among rock fragments and crevices in the limestone hills and ridges of the Big Bend region of Texas and adjacent Mexico. The U.S. Fish and Wildlife Service lists this cactus as a proposed threatened species.

Elevation: 2,500–4,000 feet

Range: Big Bend region of west Texas and north central Mexico

BUTTON CACTUS
Epithelantha micromeris

Button cactus may be solitary or clumping, with stems three inches in diameter, and short, dense, whitish spines. Emerging at the stem tips, the flowers are whitish to pink, followed by erect, slender, bright red fruits. Button cactus is widespread in limestone or igneous soils of rocky hills and ridges in desert and grasslands of the Chihuahuan Desert. Five subspecies of *E. micromeris* are currently recognized.

This species is popular with hobbyists and widely grown in private collections.

Elevation: 3,400–5,000 feet

Range: Eastern Arizona, New Mexico and west Texas; Coahuila, San Luis Potosi, and Nuevo Leon, Mexico

BEEHIVE CACTUS
Escobaria vivipara (Coryphantha vivipara)

Beehive is a low, clustering species, with globose stems growing only three to five inches high. The stout, central spines are orange to brown, with white radials. Bright pink to violet flowers with pointed tips emerge near the top of the stem, followed by half-inch to one-inch green, scaly fruits. Beehive cactus is found in a variety of habitats throughout a broad elevational and geographic range throughout the West. As many as eight varieties have been recognized, but their taxonomic status is unclear.

Elevation: 600–9,000 feet

Range: Widespread in the western U.S. and Canada

SPINY BARREL
(Fire Barrel, California Barrel)
Ferocactus cylindraceus (F. acanthodes)

Spiny barrel is typically cylindrical in shape and rarely branching. The four to seven central spines vary in color and may be white, red, yellow, or brown. Spines may be curved or slightly hooked, and round or flattened in cross section. Radial spines intergrade with the centrals. Light yellow flowers emerge in a ring at the stem tips in spring. The yellow fruits are spineless and round, releasing seeds through basal pores. Spiny barrel typically grows on steep, rocky slopes in the Mojave and Sonoran deserts.

Subspecies *cylindraceus* has twisted yellow, red, or brown central spines, fifteen to twenty-five radials and can grow to ten feet tall. It occurs in southern California and southwestern Arizona, and northern Baja and northwestern Sonora, Mexico. Subspecies *lecontei* does not have twisted or hooked spines and occurs in southern Nevada, southwestern Utah, southern California, and much of Arizona. Subspecies *tortulospinus* has shorter stems, often flattened tips, and twisted gray spines. It occurs only in northern Baja California, Mexico.

Elevation: 1,000–5,000 feet

Range: Southern California, Nevada, Utah, and Arizona; Baja California and Sonora, Mexico

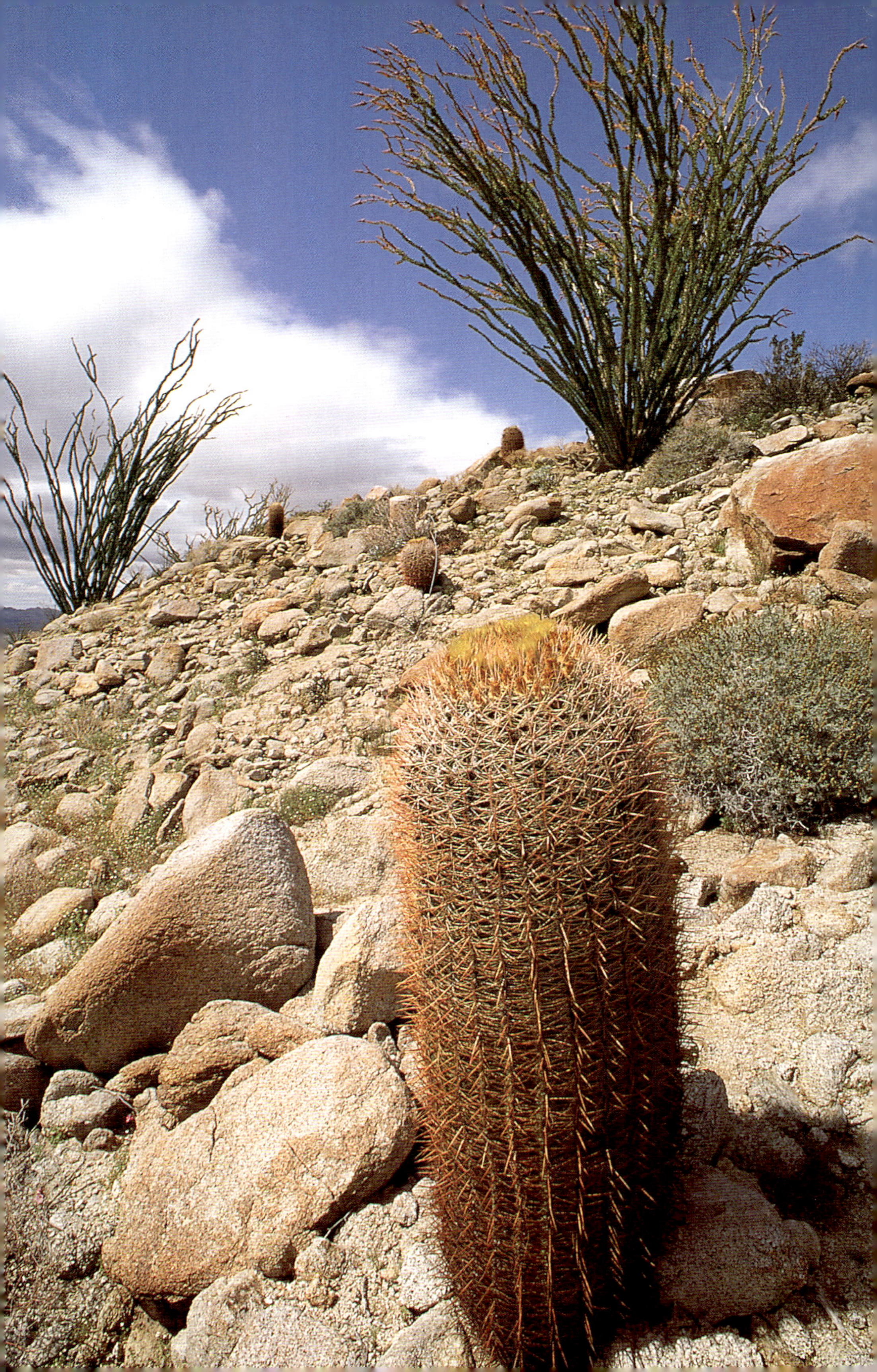

ssp. emoryi

EMORY'S BARREL
(Coville's Barrel, Bisnaga)
Ferocactus emoryi (F. covillei)

Plants are solitary, globose to cylindrical, growing up to eight feet tall and three and a half feet in diameter. One very stout, straight, curved or hooked central spine and few radials are present. Large, showy flowers ring the stem tips in summer and may be yellow, mahogany red, or a mixture of both. Emory's barrel occurs in rocky or gravelly soils on hillsides, mesas and desert flats.

Subspecies *emoryi* grows to eight feet in height with thirty or more ribs, and occurs in Arizona, and Sonora and Sinaloa, Mexico. Subspecies *rectispinus* grows to five feet with twenty-one ribs; has unusually long, straight spines; and occurs only in northern Baja California, Mexico.

Emerging central spines of *Ferocactus emoryi* have been used by the Seri to make rose-colored face paint.

Elevation: 1,500–3,000 feet

Range: Southern Arizona; Sonora, Sinaloa, and Baja California, Mexico

FIRE BARREL (Bisnaga Colorada)
Ferocactus gracilis

Fire barrel is a solitary plant growing to five feet tall and is immediately recognizable because of its bright orange-red spines. The central spines are red with yellow tips, the main four forming a cross, with the upper and lower ones flattened. Deep red flowers emerge in early summer, followed by oblong yellow fruits. Fire barrel is endemic to Baja California, Mexico, and occurs on rocky hillsides, flats, and bajadas. Three subspecies are recognized.

Subspecies *gracilis* grows to three feet or more with spines less than a quarter-inch wide, and occurs in north central Baja. Subspecies *coloratus* rarely reaches three feet in height, has centrals that often are wider than a quarter inch, and occurs in an area south of, and slightly overlapping, subspecies *gracilis*. The uncommon subspecies *gatesii* can grow to five feet high, has curved central spines that are only one-eighth-inch wide, and occurs on the islands near Bahia de los Angeles.

Elevation: below 3,000 feet

Range: Baja California, Mexico

ssp. coloratus

TEXAS BARREL
Ferocactus hamatacanthus

The Texas barrel is usually solitary, growing to two feet high and a foot in diameter, with mostly brownish-red spines. The thin, hooked and straw-colored or orange-red central spines, up to eight inches long, are a distinguishing feature of this species. Flowers are showy, yellow, or yellow with red centers, clustering at the top of the stem. Small fruits, one to two inches wide, ripen to a reddish brown color. Texas barrel is found on gravelly soils in desert and grassland in the Chihuahuan Desert.

Subspecies *hamatacanthus* has stems to two feet high, four to eight central spines, and yellow flowers with red centers. It occurs in southeastern New Mexico, southwestern Texas, and northern Mexico. Subspecies *sinuatus* grows to only a foot tall, has four central spines and yellow flowers, and occurs in southeast Texas and northern Mexico. Flower buds, or *cabuches*, of *F. hamatcanthus* are harvested commercially in San Luis Potosi, Mexico. They are cooked and added to salads, soups, and other dishes.

ssp. sinuatus

Elevation: Near sea level–5,000 feet

Range: New Mexico and Texas; and north central Mexico

COAST BARREL
Ferocactus viridescens

The coast barrel is inconspicuous due to its small size, growing to only about a foot high and wide, with a globose or cylindrical shape. Spines can be reddish or golden yellow, eventually turning gray as the plant ages. The four to nine central spines are curved, and radials are stout or bristle-like. Greenish yellow flowers—each two and a half inches wide—bloom in summer and are followed by light green or red globular fruits. Coast barrel is found only in sandy or gravelly soils of the coastal chaparral vegetation of southwestern California and northwestern Baja California.

Elevation: 30–500 feet

Range: Southern California and northern Baja California, Mexico

FISHHOOK BARREL (Compass Barrel)
Ferocactus wislizeni

Fishhook barrel is a solitary plant, usually globose but sometimes cylindrical. Four central spines form a cross, the lower ones stout and usually strongly hooked. Satiny, brilliant orange but sometimes yellow or red flowers crown the plants in late summer, followed by lemon yellow, spineless fruits that resemble small pineapples. Fruits may persist for a year unless consumed by birds, squirrels, or large mammals.

It is the largest barrel cactus found in the U.S., with mature ones reaching eight to ten feet tall and living about a century. Fishhook barrel tends to lean toward the southwest. It may be that growth occurs more quickly on the cooler side of the plant. Fishhook barrel favors rocky, sandy, or gravelly soils on low hills and flats in deserts and grasslands.

The Seri and Tohono O'odham obtained emergency liquid by cutting, pounding, and squeezing the pulp. The Pima used the central spines as fishhooks, and also removed the top and spines, cutting the fleshy core into slices, and boiling it with mesquite beans.

Elevation: 1,000–5,600 feet

Range: Central and southern Arizona, southern New Mexico, and southwestern Texas; northwestern Mexico

PEYOTE CACTUS
Lophophora williamsii

Solitary or forming low clumps, peyote cactus has blue-green, fleshy and spineless, button-like stems, with thick, tapered roots. Wispy tufts of white hair occur on the tubercles. Delicate, pale pink to white, half-inch-wide flowers emerge from within the woolly areoles at the center of the stems. The club-shaped or elongated fruits are pinkish red, ripening to tan.

Peyote cactus has a long history of use in religious and ceremonial practices. The Huichol and Tarahumara of Mexico have traditionally made pilgrimages to peyote sites to collect plants for ceremonial use. Peyote contains more than fifty alkaloids, including mescaline. When ingested, peyote causes one to experience vivid colors and an enhancement of the senses. The use of peyote in religious ceremonies spread to Native Americans in the U.S. in the middle of the nineteenth century. Today more than a quarter million Native Americans belong to the Native American Church, in which peyote is eaten as the sacrament.

Elevation: 160–5,900 feet

Range: West and south Texas; northern Mexico to San Luis Potosi

CALIFORNIA FISHHOOK CACTUS
Mammillaria dioica

California fishhook is solitary or clustering, to about a foot high, with three-inch-wide stems. Central spines (sometimes absent) are brownish black and needle-like, with the lower one hooked and upper ones straight. Radial spines are needle-like and white. The cactus blooms in spring and summer and the flowers are white to yellowish white with green stigma lobes. Flowers are followed by crimson club-shaped or oval fruits. California fishhook is extremely common throughout Mexico's Baja peninsula and is typically found in rocky, gravelly, or sandy soils on hillsides or in washes, in chaparral, or desert vegetation.

Elevation: 50–5,000 feet

Range: Southern California and Baja California, Mexico

PINCUSHION CACTUS
(Arizona Fishhook Cactus)
Mammillaria grahamii (M. microcarpa)

Pincushion cactus is solitary or branching, with light green stems that grow to eight inches high and four inches wide. Central spines are dark brown, and the longest one is usually hooked. Showy flowers to two inches wide occur in a ring around the tip of the stems, and bloom intermittently throughout the summer rainy season. The tasty, edible fruits are slender, red-orange pods. Pincushion cactus is typically found under small shrubs in sandy or gravelly soils in desert or desert grassland. The Seri and the Pima removed the spines and cooked the plant as a treatment for earache.

Elevation: 1,000–5,000 feet

Range: California, Arizona, New Mexico, and Texas; Sonora, Sinaloa, and Chihuahua, Mexico

CREAM CACTUS
Mammillaria heyderi (M. macdougalii)

Plants are solitary, with flattened stems up to eight inches wide containing milky latex. The dark, straight central spines are about a half-inch in length, while radials are bristly and white. Flower color can range from cream to brownish pink, with reddish fruits. During times of drought, cream cactus often will shrink to below soil level. Cream cactus is an extremely wide-ranging species and occurs in desert and grassland, thornscrub, and woodland from the southwestern U.S. to the Yucatan Peninsula in Mexico. Six subspecies are recognized. The milky latex in the plant is used by the Tarahumara to treat ear pain and deafness.

Elevation: Sea level–5,300 feet

Range: Texas, Arizona, southern New Mexico, and southwest Oklahoma; throughout Mexico south to the Yucatan Peninsula

LACESPINE PINCUSHION
Mammillaria lasiacantha

Lacespine pincushion is typically solitary and notable for its small size, with stems only about one and a half inches in diameter. Delicate, white to pinkish spines are dense and numerous, sometimes with soft, lacey hairs. The half-inch-wide flowers vary from white to green with distinct red or brown midveins on the petaloids. Fruits are scarlet and oval to club-shaped. In Texas, lacespine cactus frequently grows alongside button cactus (*Epithelantha micromeris*) and is often confused with it. Both occur in limestone soils on hills and mesas. This is a wide-ranging species in the Chihuahuan Desert, with small, disjunct populations in southern Arizona and northwestern Sonora, Mexico. Three subspecies are recognized.

Elevation: 1,300–4,300 feet

Range: Arizona, New Mexico, and west Texas; Coahuila, Chihuahua, Durango, and Zacatecas, Mexico

CORKY-SEED PINCUSHION
Mammillaria tetrancistra

A solitary or clumping species, corky-seed pincushion has tuberous roots and three to four brown or black central spines, with the lower one hooked. Dense radial spines are white, or white with dark tips. Rose, orchid, or lavender-pink flowers—each an inch and a half wide—circle the stem tips with a crown of blooms in spring and summer. Each petal is edged with white. Slender, bright red fruits contain the distinctive black, pitted seeds with corky bases. Corky-seed pincushion occurs in sandy soils on hillsides and flats of the Mojave and Sonoran deserts.

Elevation: 450–2,400 feet

Range: California, Arizona, Nevada, and Utah; northern Baja California and Sonora, Mexico

CLUSTERED PINCUSHION
Mammillaria thornberi

Clustered pincushion is distinctive with its very slender stems and clustering habit. One pale to reddish brown, strongly hooked central spine is present, along with numerous white or yellow radials with dark tips. Flowering in midsummer, the blooms are pale pink to lavender pink with very conspicuous deep pink stigmas. Fruits are plump and bright red. Subspecies *yaquensis* has half-inch-diameter stems, pubescent (hairy) radials, and occurs only along the west coast of central Sonora, Mexico. Subspecies *thornberi* has inch-diameter stems, non-pubescent radials, and occurs in southern Arizona and northern Sonora. Clustered pincushion commonly occurs under shrubs in sandy or fine soils of desert flats and washes in the Sonoran Desert.

Elevation: Sea level–2,400 feet

Range: Southern Arizona and Sonora, Mexico

ssp. thornberi

ssp. wilcoxii

WRIGHT'S PINCUSHION
Mammillaria wrightii

The solitary stems of Wright's pincushion are dark green, one to three inches in diameter, with dark, hooked central spines and white radials. Brilliant magenta to purple flowers emerge in a ring around the stem, followed by spherical, purplish fruits. Wright's pincushion is widespread in the Southwest and occurs in desert grassland and oak and pinyon-juniper woodland. Subspecies *wrightii* has large magenta flowers, inch-diameter fruits, and occurs widely in New Mexico, and Sonora and Chihuahua, Mexico. Subspecies *wilcoxii* has bright purple or white flowers and is found in southeastern Arizona and southwestern New Mexico, and Sonora and Chihuahua.

Elevation: 3,000–8,000 feet

Range: New Mexico and Arizona; the Sierra Madre of northern Mexico

COCHAL
Myrtillocactus cochal

A shrubby to treelike columnar cactus that grows up to ten feet high, cochal forms a candelabra-like arrangement of blue-green stems on a short trunk. Typically, a single black, inch-long central spine is present, with few gray or black radials. Small, green to white flowers open day and night intermittently throughout the year, and then develop into round, red, marble-sized, edible fruits. Cochal is endemic to Baja California and is found on hillsides, mesas and canyons in localities throughout the peninsula. This handsome cactus is often cultivated in desert gardens, as is the related *Myrtillocactus geometrizans*.

Elevation: Sea level–3,500 feet

Range: Baja California, Mexico

BEAVERTAIL CACTUS
Opuntia basilaris

An attractive, low-growing, blue-green prickly pear, beavertail cactus is usually free of large spines, though tiny glochids are plentiful. Growing to a height of only about twenty inches, it will form low, dense clumps up to seven feet wide under optimum conditions. Emerging in early to late spring, the large and showy flowers range from deep pink to cherry red. Fruits are dry and tan or gray at maturity. Beavertail cactus is common in the Mojave and Sonoran deserts and associated grassland and woodland vegetation. The Shoshoni make a poultice from the pads to apply to cuts and wounds as a pain remedy. This attractive and compact prickly pear is widely cultivated in desert gardens.

Elevation: Sea level–9,000 feet

Range: California, Nevada, Arizona, and Utah; Sonora, Mexico

PANCAKE PRICKLY PEAR
Opuntia chlorotica

Pancake prickly pear is a shrubby or tree-like species that grows from three to seven feet in height, often with stout trunks. Pads are usually quite round, blue-green to yellow-green in color, and range from nearly spineless to densely covered with shaggy, golden yellow spines. Flowers are pale yellow with a tinge of red, followed by grayish purple, fleshy fruits. Pancake prickly pear is typically found in rocky or sandy soils on steep, rocky slopes, in canyons, and occasionally in desert flats in Mojave and Sonoran desert localities

Elevation: 2000–6,000 feet

Range: California, Nevada, Utah, Arizona and New Mexico; Baja California and Sonora, Mexico

ENGELMANN'S PRICKLY PEAR
Opuntia engelmannii (O. phaeacantha discata)

Shrubby with sprawling or upright branches, Engelmann's prickly pear can grow to eleven feet in height, although more typical specimens are four to six feet tall. Pads are oval to round, five to eight inches wide, with extremely variable spines. The large flowers—usually bright yellow, then fading to peach or light red—bloom in late spring and are followed by purple to burgundy, plump, edible fruits. Six varieties of *O. engelmannii* are recognized.

Young cooked pads, called *nopalitos*, are a traditional food of the Tohono O'odham and other southwestern tribes. Recent studies have shown that this food can significantly lower cholesterol and blood sugar levels in diabetic individuals. Prickly pear fruits also have been an important staple and have been found to have similar nutritional benefits. Fruits traditionally were harvested with tongs and brushed with grass or rolled on the ground to remove glochids. They could then be peeled and eaten raw or sun-dried and stored.

The Pima applied heated pads to a new mother's breasts to stimulate the flow of milk.

Elevation: Sea level– 5,000 feet

Range: Widely distributed in Arizona, New Mexico, Texas, Oklahoma, and Louisiana; northern and central Mexico

INDIAN FIG CACTUS (Nopal)
Opuntia ficus-indica

Individual plants of the treelike, usually spineless, Indian fig cactus can grow up to twenty feet tall with well developed trunks over a foot in diameter. The thick pads vary in shape and can be one to two feet long. Yellow-orange to red flowers bloom in late spring, followed by fruits that ripen to green or pale red.

Indigenous people of Mexico selected horticultural and hybrid forms of this species and used them for a variety of purposes. The fruits, or *tunas*, were made into a syrup or jam; a tea of the flowers was used as a treatment for kidney problems. Sliced and cooked pads, or *nopales*, were consumed as a nutritious vegetable. *Miel de tuna*, or prickly pear honey, was made by boiling mashed pulp from which the seeds have been removed. Fruits and pads are still popular food items in Mexico and the Southwest.

Indian fig cactus was planted at the early missions of coastal California and became known as the mission cactus. The fruits and pads were eaten, and the mucilage from the pads was used to strengthen adobe bricks from which new mission churches were constructed. The cactus soon escaped from cultivation, however, and has naturalized in many parts of California and Baja California, Mexico, and hybridized with populations of native *Opuntia* species.

Range: Due to widespread cultivation over many years, the true origin of the species is not known. It is thought to have originated in central Mexico.

PURPLE PRICKLY PEAR
Opuntia gosseliniana (O. santa-rita *var.* gosseliniana)

An upright cactus branching at the base and growing up to three and a half feet high, purple prickly pear has round to teardrop-shaped, blue or purple pads. Yellow to reddish spines—two to four inches long—may be present or absent. Showy, three-inch-wide, bright yellow flowers are followed by oval, purplish fruits. Although similar to Santa Rita prickly pear, *O. gosseliniana* is a smaller plant with a more compact growth form. It is found in sandy or gravelly soils in the Sonoran and Chihuahuan deserts in and associated grasslands.

Elevation: 3,000–4,000 feet

Range: Baja California, Sonora, and Chihuahua, Mexico

SPINELESS PRICKLY PEAR
Opuntia laevis (O. phaeacantha *var.* laevis)

Shrubby and virtually free of spines, *O. laevis* has few branches and grows from three to six and a half feet in height. The three-inch-wide, lemon yellow flowers are followed by cylindrical fruits two to three inches long. This unarmed species is able to survive by growing in inaccessible habitats such as rocky ledges and crevices on cliffs and steep canyon walls, where it is are protected from grazing animals. Rodents also will feed on the plant during prolonged drought. Spineless prickly pear occurs in desert, grassland, and oak woodland vegetation.

Elevation: 2,500–3,500 feet

Range: Central and southern Arizona

COAST PRICKLY PEAR
Opuntia littoralis

Coast prickly pear can be sprawling or upright, one to two feet high, and often forms dense colonies. Pads are elliptical to round, up to a foot long and four inches wide, with brown, gray, or gold spines. The three-inch-wide flowers range from yellow to red or magenta and are followed by fleshy, reddish purple fruits. Coast prickly pear is found on coastal bluffs and hillsides in chaparral vegetation.

Elevation: Near sea level–2,000 feet, with some populations to 4,000 feet

Range: Southern California and northern Baja California, Mexico

LONG-SPINED PRICKLY PEAR
Opuntia macrocentra (O. santa-rita *var.* macrocentra)

Long-spined prickly pear is low or shrubby, growing up to about three feet in height with dark green to blue-green pads. The distinctive long spines are black to reddish brown with white tips, and are most abundant on or just below the edge of the pad. In late spring, bright yellow flowers with scarlet red centers emerge, followed by small, purple-red fruits.

Variety *macrocentra* has dark green to purple pads, six to eight inches wide, and purplish red fruits. This variety is found is Arizona, New Mexico, and Texas. Variety *minor* has blue-green pads four to six inches wide and pinkish red fruits. It occurs in the Big Bend region of Texas and adjacent Mexico. Both varieties are found in desert or desert grassland vegetation.

var. macrocentra

Elevation: 2,000–5,500 feet

Range: Arizona, New Mexico, and Texas; Sonora, Mexico

PLAINS PRICKLY PEAR
(Tuberous-Rooted Prickly Pear)
Opuntia macrorhiza

Plains prickly pear forms low, sprawling clumps up to six and a half feet wide and about five inches high, with fleshy, tuberous roots. The thick, often wrinkled pads are round to obovate, and have straight or curving spines. Bright yellow flowers with red centers bloom in spring and summer, followed by purple or reddish fleshy fruits. A wide-ranging, cold-hardy species found throughout the Plains States and the Southwest, plains prickly pear grows in desert, grassland, woodland and montane forest.

Variety *macrorhiza* has pads up to four inches long with yellow (or yellow with red centers) flowers, and occurs widely throughout the range of the species. Variety *pottsii* has pads to just two and one half inches long, reddish flowers, and occurs only in west Texas, New Mexico, and Arizona. The pads of plains prickly pear have been roasted by the Navajo to make a liniment to aid in childbirth. Spines are used to lance infections.

Elevation: 500–8,000 feet

Range: Plains States and Southwest U.S.

var. macrorhiza

BROWN-SPINED PRICKLY PEAR
Opuntia phaeacantha

Brown-spined prickly pear is a widespread and variable species that is prostrate, sprawling or upright, often forming clumps to three feet high and eight feet wide. Pads can be obovate to nearly round, with reddish brown to dark brown spines that are straight, curved, or twisted. Emerging in late spring, the large, showy flowers are commonly lemon yellow, sometimes with reddish centers, and are followed by reddish purple to burgundy fruits. As many as ten varieties of *O. phaeacantha* have been recognized in the U.S. and seven in Mexico. The species occurs in habitats ranging from low desert to montane forest. The Seri created red face paint by crushing fruits of *O. phaeacantha*. The Pima placed heated pads on the breasts of new mothers to encourage the flow of milk.

Elevation: 1,250–8,000 feet

Range: Widely distributed in the southwestern U.S. and northern Mexico

BLIND PRICKLY PEAR
Opuntia rufida

Blind prickly pear is a shrubby, upright cactus that grows to about five feet tall, with very round, spineless, blue-green to gray-green pads up to eight inches wide. Dense clusters of reddish brown glochids dot the pads. The three-inch-wide, bright yellow flowers fade to a pale orange hue and are followed by dull red, fleshy, oblong fruits. Blind prickly pear is a Chihuahuan Desert species that occurs in sandy or gravelly soils along washes or on rocky hillsides. This species is notorious for releasing glochids when disturbed, and these have been known to blind cattle, hence the common name.

Elevation: 2,000–3,500 feet

Range: West Texas; Chihuahua and Coahuila, Mexico

SANTA RITA PRICKLY PEAR
Opuntia santa-rita

Santa Rita prickly pear is an upright, shrubby plant that will form stands up to ten feet wide and six and a half feet high. Stunning, violet-purple pads are very round and have a spineless appearance, although one to three spines per areole are often present. The three-inch-wide bright yellow flowers are followed by fleshy purple or red fruits. This species is typically found on gravelly or rocky hillsides in the Sonoran and Chihuahuan deserts, associated grassland, and oak woodland. The non-spiny appearance and rich coloration of the pads have made this a highly desirable and widely cultivated cactus in Southwest desert gardens and landscapes.

Elevation: 3,000–5,000 feet

Range: Southeastern Arizona and southern New Mexico; northern Sonora, Mexico

HECHO (Hairbrush Cactus)
Pachycereus pecten-aboriginum

Hecho cactus is a treelike, columnar cactus growing to twenty-six feet tall with a well-defined main trunk. The upright stems are deep green with ten to twelve ribs. Older stems are covered with reddish brown wool and bristles. The cactus blooms in late spring, and the sturdy white blossoms are open in the daylight hours and are pollinated by nectar-feeding bats. Hecho cactus is common in the tropical deciduous forests of Sonora and Sinaloa, Mexico, and the southern Sonoran Desert in Sonora, Mexico.

The unique fruits are covered with dense reddish bristles, and indigenous people of Mexico have used them as hairbrushes. Hecho fruits are also edible and their juice is often made into tasty syrup. The Tarahumara have used hecho cactus to make a drink that causes dizziness and hallucinations. Today, in parts of Mexico, the strong, woody skeletons of this species are used for making furniture.

Elevation: Sea level–3,000 feet

Range: Widely distributed in Baja California Sur, Sinaloa, and Sonora, Mexico

CARDÓN
Pachycereus pringlei

The largest columnar cactus in the Sonoran Desert, cardon is the giant of southwestern cacti. Its massive size, soaring to sixty feet tall with stout, upright stems and a well-developed main trunk, make this cactus unmistakable. The white, three-inch-long, funnel-shaped flowers have a fruity smell and are pollinated primarily by nectar-feeding bats.

Upon ripening, the round, edible fruits are covered with light brown felt and bristles. Traditionally, these fruits were extensively harvested and consumed by the Seri along the coast of Sonora, Mexico, using long poles similar to those used by the Tohono O'odham to gather saguaro fruits. The unusually large seeds were toasted and ground into a mash. Stem sections were used as a poultice for rheumatism and general aches and pains. According to accounts from early missionaries, the indigenous people of Baja California, Mexico, also harvested and consumed the tasty, nutritious fruits.

Elevation: Sea level–1,500 feet

Range: Coastal Sonora and the Baja Peninsula, Mexico

SENITA (Garambullo)
Pachycereus (Lophocereus) schottii

A columnar gray-green cactus that grows to about thirteen feet tall, senita branches from the base, similar to organ pipe cactus, and often forms dense thickets. Stems have four to thirteen ribs that are rimmed with short spines. Masses of long, drooping gray spines form on the branch tips of mature individuals. Delicate, funnel-shaped, pale pink flowers open at night and are pollinated by a specific type of moth, which has a mutualistic relationship with the plant. The marble-size, burgundy fruits are spineless and edible, and have been collected and consumed by the Seri and others as a palatable, nutritious food.

forma montrosus

Senita is extremely common in desert flats and thornscrub habitats throughout much of the Sonoran Desert region. The name means "old woman" in Spanish and refers to the way branches drop to the ground and root, giving the appearance of an old woman surrounded by her children and grandchildren. It is frequently cultivated as a handsome addition to desert gardens. Totem pole cactus (*Pachycereus schottii* forma *monstrosus*) is a rare, spineless form of senita that occurs in only in a few localities in Baja California, Mexico. Its unusual sculptural form has made it popular among hobbyists, and it is widely grown in succulent nurseries.

Elevation: Sea level–2,500 feet

Range: Southern Arizona; Baja California and Sonora, Mexico

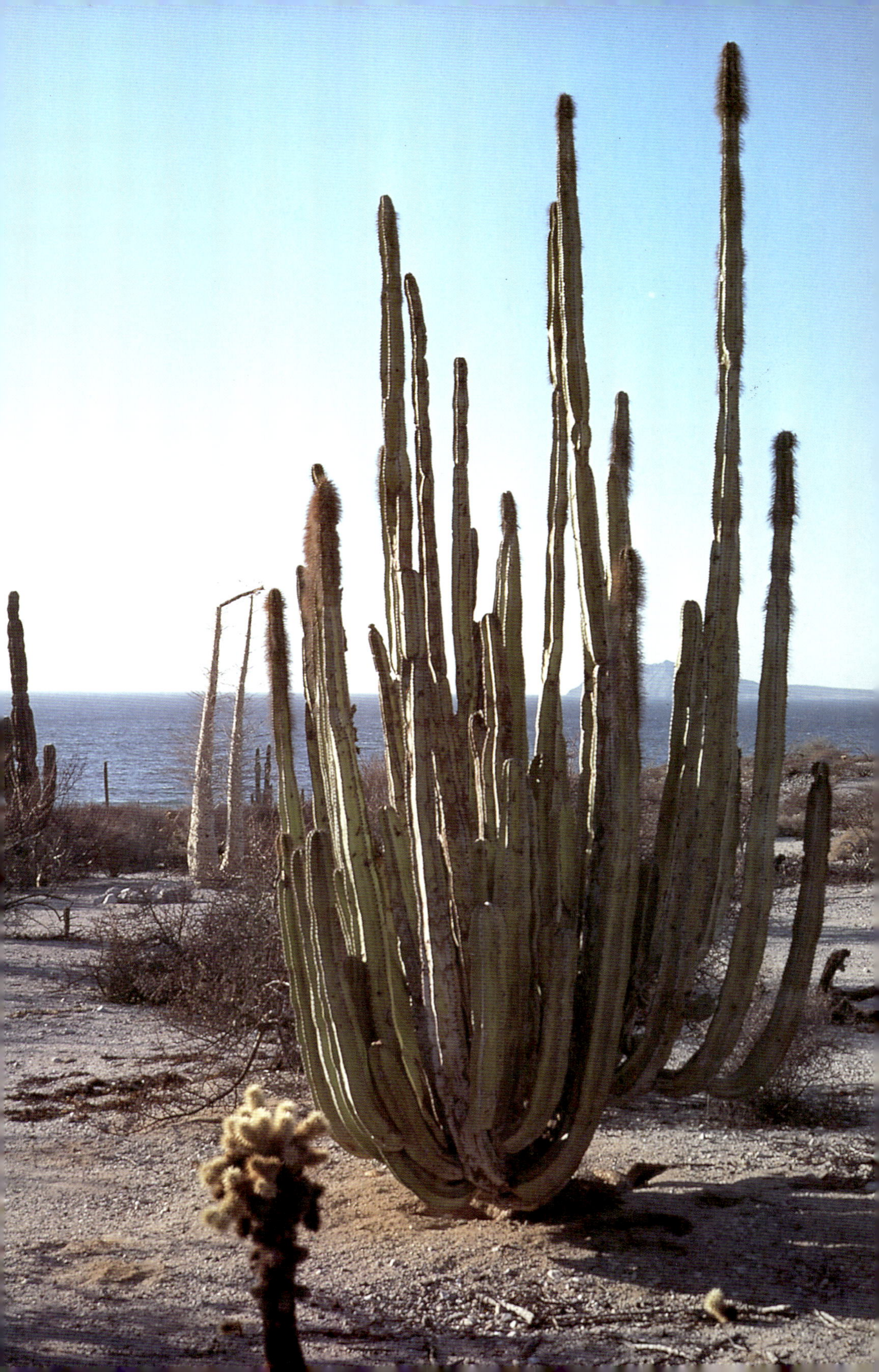

QUEEN OF THE NIGHT
(Night Blooming Cereus)
Peniocereus greggii

The upright or sprawling, slender, gray green stems of the queen of the night can grow to ten feet in length, with four to six ribs. Inconspicuous and sometimes dead-looking, the plant grows among, and is often concealed by, other desert shrubs or trees. Underground stems of older plants will form huge, edible tubers weighing up to forty pounds. In midsummer, the large, lovely, heavily perfumed flowers open at night and are pollinated by hawkmoths. Often entire populations will bloom on a single night. The upright, tapered fruits mature to a brilliant red and are two to four inches in length.

Variety *greggii* occurs only in the Chihuahuan Desert above 3,900 feet and bears two-inch-wide flowers. Variety *transmontanus* has flowers to three inches and occurs in the Sonoran Desert below 3,300 feet.

The Pima and Tohono O'odham have baked, peeled, and eaten the tubers and chewed pieces to alleviate thirst. A liquid medicine from the root also aids digestion and respiratory ailments. The tubers are now used to prevent and treat diabetes among the Pima and Tohono O'odham.

Elevation: 1,000–5,000 feet

Range: Southwest U.S. and northern Mexico

CHIHUAHUA FISHOOK CACTUS
(Cat Claw Cactus)
Sclerocactus (Ancistrocactus) uncinatus

Chihuahua fishhook cactus is usually a solitary stem that grows up to a foot in height. The distinctive, five-inch-long, central spines are hooked, tan to straw-colored, and point upward. Attractive, reddish brown, funnel-shaped flowers emerge at the stem tips in spring, followed by small, scaly fruits. This Chihuahuan Desert species is found on limestone hills and alluvial fans.

Subspecies *uncinatus*, which has one hooked central spine that points outward, occurs only in Mexico. Subspecies *crassihamatus* has five central spines and eight radials and is found only in the Mexican state of Querétero. The most northern subspecies, *wrightii*, has a single, upward-pointing central spine with eight to ten radials, and occurs in west Texas and northern Mexico.

Elevation: 2,500–4,500 feet

Range: West Texas; Sonora, Chihuahua, and San Luis Potosi, Mexico

ssp. wrightii

PITAHAYA AGRIA
Stenocereus gummosus

Pitahaya agria plants are shrubby and semi-erect, with many sprawling stems up to five feet long. Stems often root where they touch the ground and eventually form dense thickets. White to rose-pink flowers open at night and bloom in midsummer and intermittently in response to summer rain. The large, round, red fruits are extremely palatable and pleasantly tart. The Spanish common name means "sour fruit."

The Seri of Sonora and the early inhabitants of Baja California, Mexico, extensively harvested and consumed the fruits. Stems also have been used to stupefy fish. Pitahaya agria is found in sandy, rocky and gravelly soils on hillsides, plains, and arroyos in Sonoran Desert localities.

Elevation: Below 2,000 feet

Range: Coastal Sonora and Baja California, Mexico, and adjacent islands

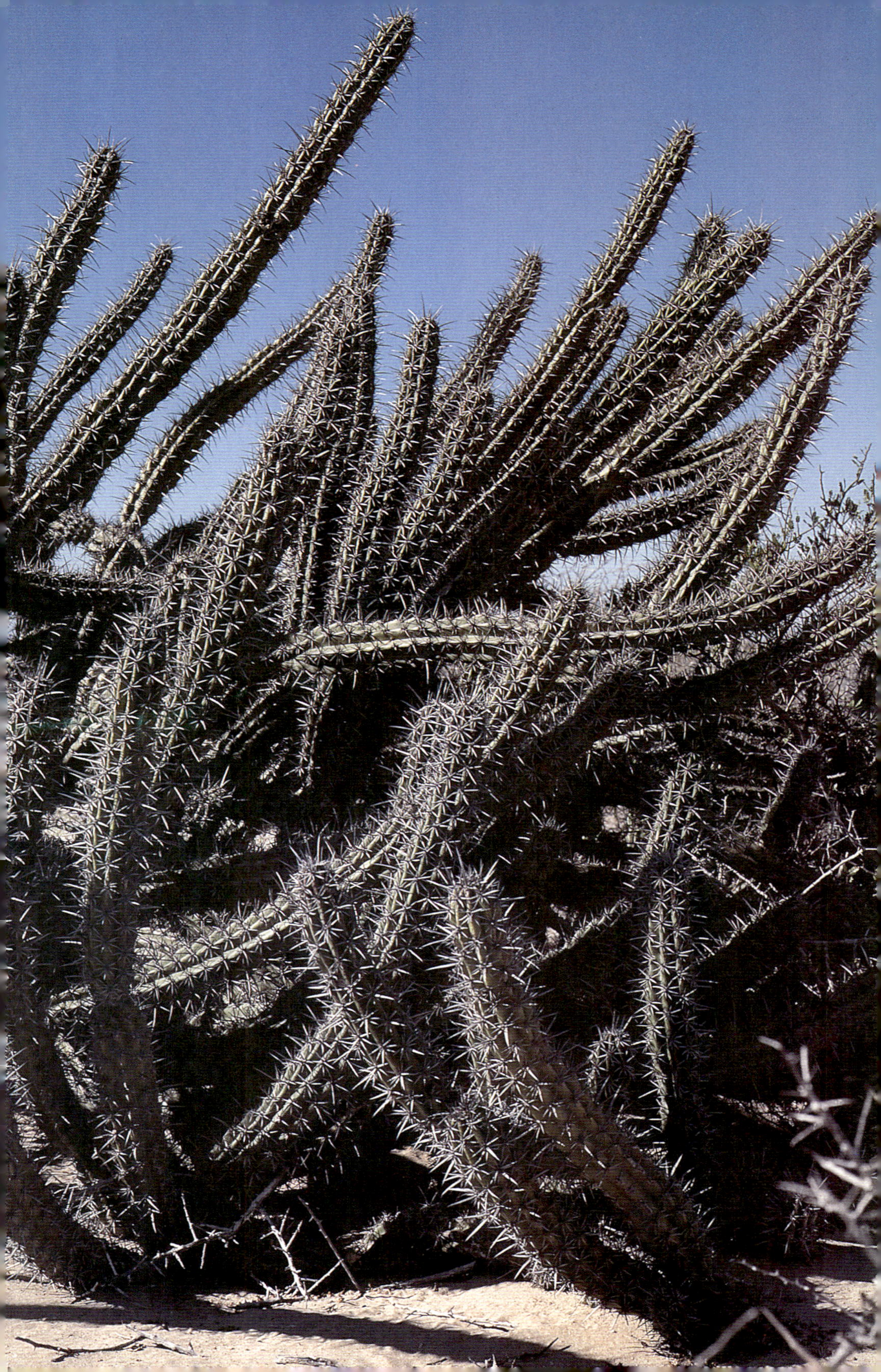

ORGAN PIPE CACTUS (Pitahaya Dulce)
Stenocereus thurberi

Organ pipe cactus is common throughout much of the Sonoran Desert, reaching its northern limit in southern Arizona, where the species tends to branch profusely from the base. In the southern parts of their range, they grow more like saguaros, forming branches higher up on a central trunk. Plants can reach up to twenty-six feet in height. The stems are a rich green color with grayish or dark, reddish brown spines. Pinkish white, funnel-shaped, nocturnal flowers are born near the stem tips in midsummer, and are pollinated primarily by nectar-feeding bats. Subspecies *littoralis* has pink flowers, reaches a maximum height of ten feet, and occurs only at the southern tip of Mexico's Baja Peninsula.

The Spanish name for organ pipe cactus, pitahaya dulce, means "sweet fruit." The round, spiny fruits are among the sweetest and best-tasting of all Sonoran Desert cacti. Pima, Tohono O'odham, Seri, Yaqui, Mayo, Opata, and Tarahumara peoples traditionally harvested and traded these fruits. The Tohono O'odham make a syrup and jam from the fruits, and dried fruits are stored for use in the winter months. Organ pipe fruits were also an extremely important food source for the indigenous people of Baja California.

Elevation: Below 3,900 feet

Range: Southern Arizona; southwestern Chihuahua, Sonora, Baja California, and Sinaloa, Mexico

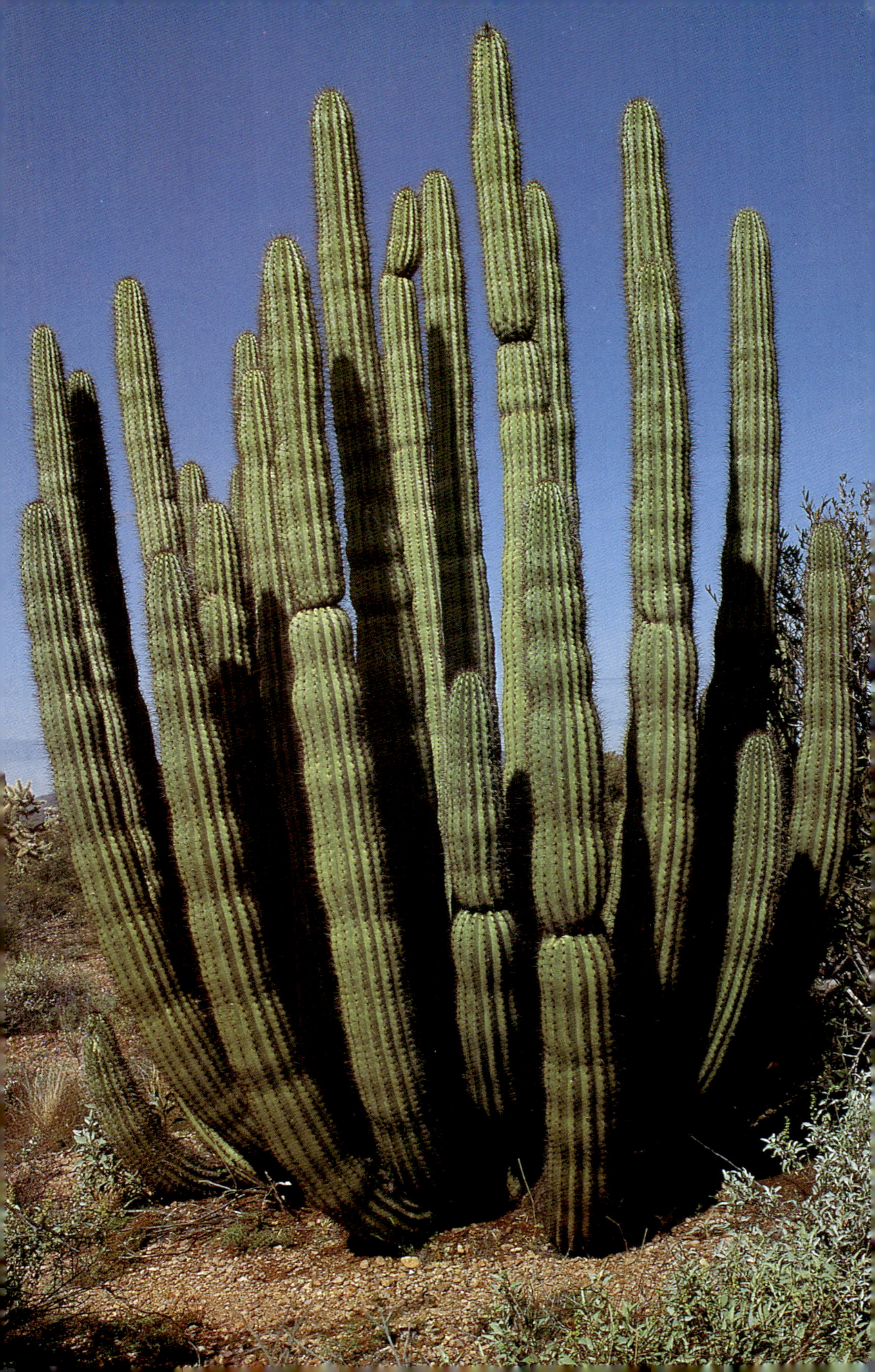

GLORY OF TEXAS
(Straw Spine Cactus)
Thelocactus bicolor

Glory of Texas is a solitary plant with a globose or elongated stem up to eight inches in height. Ribs often will form a spiral around the stem. Central spines are white to reddish and three or more inches in length. The flowers are very showy and appear at the stem tips in spring and early summer. Individual blooms may be four inches wide, are usually bright rosy-pink, with a rich scarlet throat. Fruits are green and dry at maturity.

T. bicolor is common throughout much of the Chihuahuan desert; three subspecies are recognized. Subspecies *bicolor* has one to four central spines, eight to fifteen radials, and occurs widely throughout the Chihuahuan Desert and Tamaulipan thrornscrub along the Rio Grande.

Subspecies *flavidispinus* is very densely spined, has three centrals and twelve to seventeen radials, and is restricted hard rock outcrops in the Chihuahuan desert of Texas and, possibly, Mexico. Subspecies *schwarzii* has tri-colored flowers, no centrals, thirteen to fourteen radials, and is restricted to thornscrub vegetation in Tamaulipas east of the Sierra Madre Oriental.

Elevation: Sea level–6,000 feet

Range: Texas and northern Mexico

ssp. bicolor

GLOSSARY

Areole–specialized structure producing leaves, spines, and flowers

Central spine–one of the innermost spines of an areole

Fruit–derived from the ovary following fertilization and development of seeds within

Glochid–tiny, barbed spine, often occurring in tufts

Habitat–locality with certain ecological characteristics where an organism occurs

Hybrid–an individual resulting from the crossing of two different taxa

Joint–a stem segment of cholla

Ovary–lower part of the pistil containing the ovules; becomes the fruit following fertilization

Pad–a stem segment of prickly pear

Perianth parts–used when petals and sepals are not readily distinguished

Pollination–transfer of pollen from flower to flower

Radial spine–one of the outermost spines of an areole

Stigma–terminal portion of the pistil that receives pollen during pollination

Succulent–a plant that stores water in leaves, stems, or roots

Tubercle–a protuberance from the stem, usually bearing the areole

Tuber–fleshy underground portion of a stem

INDEX

Ariocarpus fissuratus 1
Arizona fishhook cactus 55
Arizona rainbow 35
Astrophytum asterias 2
Beavertail cactus 62
Beehive cactus 45
Bergerocactus emoryi 3
Bisnaga (see Emory's barrel)
Bisnaga colorada 49
Blind prickly pear 74
Blue barrel 22
Boke button cactus 43
Bonker hedgehog 25
Brown-flowered hedgehog 38
Brown-spined prickly pear 71
Buckhorn cholla 10
Button cactus 44
California barrel 46
California fishhook cactus 54
Cane cholla 20
Cardon 75
Carnegiea gigantea 4-5
Cat claw cactus 79
Chain fruit cholla 15
Chihuahua fishhook cactus 79
Chihuahua pineapple cactus 39
Chisos mountain hedgehog 26
Christmas cholla 17
Claret cup cactus 37
Clustered pincushion 59
Coast barrel 51
Coast prickly pear 68
Coastal cholla 18
Cochal 61
Compass barrel 52
Corky-seed pincushion 58
Coryphantha echinus 6
Coryphantha macromeris 7
Coryphantha recurvata 8
Coryphantha robustispina 9
Coryphantha vivipara
    (see *Escobaria vivipara*)

Coville's barrel 48
Cream cactus 56
Cylindropuntia acanthocarpa 10
Cylindropuntia arbuscula 11
Cylindropuntia bigelovii 12-13
Cylindropuntia echinocarpa 14
Cylindropuntia fulgida 15
Cylindropuntia imbricata 16
Cylindropuntia leptocaulis 17
Cylindropuntia prolifera 18
Cylindropuntia ramosissima 19
Cylindropuntia spinosior 20
Cylindropuntia versicolor 21
Diamond cholla 19
Eagle claw 22
Echinocactus horizonthalonius 22
Echinocactus polycephalus 23
Echinocactus texensis 24
Echinocereus bonkerae 25
Echinocereus chisoensis 26
Echinocereus coccineus
    (see *Echinocereus triglochidiatus*)
Echinocereus dasyacanthus 27
Echinocereus engelmannii 28
Echinocereus engelmannii
    var. *bonkerae*
    (see *Echinocereus bonkerae*)
Echinocereus engelmannii var. *nicholii*
    (see *Echinocereus nicholii*)
Echinocereus enneacanthus 29
Echinocereus fasciculatus 30
Echinocereus fendleri 31
Echinocereus ledingii 32
Echinocereus mojavensis 33
Echinocereus nicholii 34
Echinocereus pectinatus
    var. *rigidissimus*
    (see *Echinocereus rigidissimus*)
Echinocereus pectinatus
    var. *dasyacanthus*
    (see *Echinocereus dasyacanthus*)
Echinocereus rigidissimus 35

Echinocereus stramineus 36
Echinocereus triglochidiatus 37
Echinocereus triglochidiatus
  var. *mojavensis*
  (see *Echinocereus mojavensis*)
Echinocereus viridiflorus 38
Echinomastus intertextus 39
Echinomastus johnsoni 40
Echinomastus mariposensis 41
Echinomastus warnockii 42
Emory's barrel 48
Engelmann's hedgehog 28
Engelmann's prickly pear 64
Epithelantha bokei 43
Epithelantha micromeres 44
Escobaria vivipara 45
Fendler's hedgehog 31
Ferocactus acanthodes
  (see *Ferocactus cylindraceus*)
Ferocactus covillei
  (see *Ferocactus emoryi*)
Ferocactus cylindraceus 46-47
Ferocactus emoryi 48
Ferocactus gracilis 49
Ferocactus hamatacanthus 50
Ferocactus viridescens 51
Ferocactus wislizeni 52
Fire barrel 49 (also see Spiny barrel)
Fishhook barrel 52
Garambullo 76-77
Glory of Texas 84
Gold cholla 14
Golden hedgehog 34
Golden torch 3
Golden-chested beehive 8
Green-flowered hedgehog 38
Hairbrush cactus 76
Hecho 76
Horse crippler 24
Indian fig cactus 65
Johnson's pineapple cactus 40
Jumping cholla 15
Lacespine pincushion 57
Leding's hedgehog 32
Living rock cactus 1
Long mamma 7

Long-spined prickly pear 69
Lophophora williamsii 53
Mammillaria dioica 54
Mammillaria grahamii 55
Mammillaria heyderi 56
Mammillaria lasiacantha 57
Mammillaria macdougalii
  (see *Mammillaria heyderi*)
Mammillaria microcarpa
  (see *Mammillaria grahamii*)
Mammillaria tetrancistra 58
Mammillaria thornberi 59
Mammillaria wrightii 60
Many-headed barrel 23
Mariposa cactus 41
Mojave hedgehog 33
Myrtillocactus cochal 61
Night blooming cereus 78
Nopal 65
Opuntia basilaris 62
Opuntia chlorotica 63
Opuntia engelmannii 64
Opuntia ficus-indica 65
Opuntia gosseliniana 66
Opuntia laevis 67
Opuntia littoralis 68
Opuntia macrocentra 69
Opuntia macrorhiza 70
Opuntia phaeacantha 71
Opuntia phaeacantha discata
  (see *Opuntia engelmannii*)
Opuntia phaeacantha var. *laevis*
  (see *Opuntia laevis*)
Opuntia rufida 72
Opuntia santa-rita 73
Opuntia santa-rita var. *gosseliniana*
  (see *Opuntia gosseliniana*)
Opuntia santa-rita var. *macrocentra*
  (see *Opuntia macrocentra*)
Organ pipe cactus 82-83
Pachycereus pectin-aboriginum 74
Pachycereus pringlei 75
Pachycereus (Lophocereus) schottii
  76-77
Pancake prickly pear 63
Pencil cholla 11

Peniocereus greggii 78
Peyote cactus 53
Pima pineapple cactus 9
Pineapple cactus 9
Pincushion cactus 55
Pitahaya agria 80-81
Pitahaya dulce 82-83
Plains prickly pear 70
Purple prickly pear 66
Queen of the night 78
Robust hedgehog 30
Saguaro 4-5
Sand dollar 2
Santa Cruz beehive cactus 8
Santa Rita prickly pear 73
Sclerocactus (Ancistrocactus) uncinatus 79
Sea urchin cactus 6 (also see Sand Dollar)
Senita 76-77
Silver cholla 14

Spineless prickly pear 67
Spiny barrel 46
Spiny strawberry hedgehog 36
Staghorn cholla 21
Stenocereus gummosus 80-81
Stenocereus thurberi 82-83
Straw spine cactus 84
Strawberry cactus 36
Strawberry hedgehog 29 (also see Engelmann's hedgehog)
Teddy bear cholla 12
Texas barrel 50
Texas rainbow 27
Thelocactus bicolor 84
Tree cholla 16
Tuberous-rooted prickly pear 70
Turk's head cactus 22
Velvet cactus 3
Warnock cactus 42
Wright's pincushion 60

ADDITIONAL READING

Anderson, Edward. 2001. The Cactus Family. Timber Press.

Benson, Lyman. 1982. The Cacti of the United Stated and Canada. Stanford University Press.

_____.1969. *The Cacti of Arizona*. University of Arizona Press.

_____. 1969. *The Native Cacti of California*. Stanford University Press.

Evans, Doug. 1998. *Cactuses of Big Bend National Park*. University of Texas Press.

Hodgson, Wendy. 2001. *Food Plants of the Sonoran Desert*. University of Arizona Press.

Weniger, Del. 1984. *Cacti of Texas and Neighboring States*. University of Texas Press